the doors summer's gone

by Harvey Kubernik

Front cover photos by Henry Diltz
Ticket stubs courtesy of Ida Miller

Back cover color photos by Helie Robertson,
Ticket stubs courtesy of Ida Miller
Handbill courtesy of Kirk Silsbee
KHJ chart courtesy of Ray Randolph

This book became a distributed retail document owing partially to the spiritual, financial, and combined supportive efforts of S. Ti Muntarbhorn, and Carol Schofield, MsMusic Productions.

Om Mani Padme Hum.

the doors
summer's gone

by Harvey Kubernik

Otherworld Cottage Industries
Los Angeles

First Printing, February 2018

© 2018 by Harvey Kubernik

Kubernik, Harvey
The Doors Summer's Gone

1. Doors 2. Doors--History 3. Rock Musicians--United States--Biography
I. Harvey Kubernik. II. Title.

782.42

ISBN-13: 978-1-892900-0-36
ISBN-10: 1892900033

Printed in the United States of America

COPY EDITING: JOSEPH MCCOMBS
PHOTO AND ARTIFACT COORDINATION: HARVEY KUBERNIK AND GARY STROBL
FRONT AND BACK COVER CONCEPT AND DESIGN: LINDA SNYDER
BOOK LAYOUT AND DESIGN BY OTHERWORLD COTTAGE INDUSTRIES

DEDICATIONS

For Ray & Jim, Paul A. Rothchild, Dave Diamond, Ritchie Yorke, Digby Diehl, Murray Lerner, Danny Sugerman, Ben Edmonds, Arthur Lee, Tony Funches, Jeffrey Hayden, Lois Nettleton, Buddy Collette, Kenny Washington, Woody Strode, Jackie Robinson, John R. Wooden, Dick Enberg, Keith Jackson, David A. Barmack, Rick Hall, George Avakian, Dick Clark, Casey Kasem, BMR, Paul Kantner, Satchel Paige, Teddy Ballgame, Hugh Masekela, Russ Solomon, Stirling Dale Silliphant.

Special Thanks to Gary and Greg Strobl, Nurit Wilde, Joseph McCombs, Linda Snyder, Judy Pike, Gary Schneider, Nancy Rose Retchin, Kenneth Kubernik, Andrew Loog Oldham, Chris Darrow, Andrew Solt, Peter Piper, Bill Walton, Gary Pig Gold, David Leaf, Deacon, Hal Lifson, Jay Ayer, Justin Pierce, Tom and Mollie O'Neal, Greg Shaw, Jim Cherry, John Densmore, Robby Krieger, Billy James, Jac Holzman, Carol Kaye, Harry E. Northup, James Cushing & Celeste Goyer, Mark Blake, Jim Kaplan, David Kessel, BJB, Aime Elkins-McCrory, Dean the Taping Machine, Rodney Bingenheimer, Michael Jensen, David N. Pepperell, Michael Macdonald, Frank Orlando, Stevie, Wyline, Sherry and Mick, Steven Van Zandt, Gene Youngblood, Kirk Silsbee, Ray Randolph, Paul Tarnopol, Pete Mitchell, Gene Aguilera, Lonn Friend, Sarah Kramer, Don Randi, Holly, Ida Miller, Paul Body, David Dalton, Len Sousa, Anne Moore, Rob Hill, Matt King, David B. Wolfe, Jason Elzy, Robert Sherman, Lanny Waggoner, Henry Diltz, Helie Robertson, Wes Seely, Stephen Thompson, Rich Weidman, Elliott Lefko, Greg Franco, Diane Baker, Jan Alan Henderson, Barbara Berger, The Infinite Mind, Roger Steffens, Burton Cummings, Marshall & Hilda Kubernik.

Appreciation to Travis Pike who helped me navigate the ship. "Land Ho!"

v

Table of Contents:

Introduction

I was born and raised in San Francisco. I saw every band in the mid and late '60s. But when the Doors came to the city in 1967 we all knew that there was a power to them unlike the other music groups I had witnessed live.

I mean, they had a big sound for three instruments. They were like a six-piece band that played free and let the singer poet loose. The whole sonic package worked. On records and in public appearances.

I saw them a few times in 1967 and 1968. Venues like Winterland and the Fillmore. At one Winterland show he crawled around the stage as *The Jonathan Winters Show* television program was being broadcast at the same time where they did "Moonlight Drive." There was a small portable black-and-white TV sitting on a chair on the stage.

By 1968, Jim Morrison was the new bad boy on the block. A sex symbol who had that God kind of thing about him. Jim had a presence and commanded the stage. Now a rock star clad in black leather pants. And he was polite, ya know. A period before he started getting way out there. Jim bonded with the audience. It's documented on the live album. We gave the singer some and he gave us some back.

Their live show was strong. Gritty and entertaining. The Doors took you on a trip. The sound was big and large. It grabbed and sucked you in. He might have been a mess one night during "Unknown Soldier" but we all paid attention. It felt loose. He pulled it off in some weird form. It was wild, cool and interesting. The band could always pull it off in these uncontrolled circumstances. And besides, we always had the albums to return to.

I know the focus has always been on Jim. That might have started with the front cover of their debut album. But the fans and the devoted like myself and Harvey Kubernik, and so many others in our world, always knew it was a team on stage. And in the studio.

I loved Robby Krieger's guitar work and his songwriting. He made me check out some jazz albums. John Densmore, the drummer, kicked my ass. Ray Manzarek was central to the heartbeat of Jim.

And there was Morrison's writing and lyrics. Nothing like I had heard before. It was fresh. He was such a poet. It was theater. Rock 'n' roll blended with sex, Greek mythology. I mean, Jim let it rip.

The Doors have always been part of my rock 'n' roll journey.

After the Doors ended in 1971 as a physical performing act, I owned Vault of Records in the Mission district. I then worked at Tower Records in San Francisco in the early '70s. Every time I sold one of their albums to a customer, I felt I was giving them something special and essential. I later was employed by Bill Graham Winterland Productions and, in the late '80s, started E Street Records in Sacramento.

All during the '90s and through the last decade, I owned Foothill Records in La Canada, California, and continued to sell their albums on vinyl and compact disc. And on occasion, I still watch videos and DVDs on the Doors.

In 2014, Harvey Kubernik walked into Foothill Records. He was with the poet and songwriter Stephen J. Kalinich, who had once recited poetry to Jim Morrison and Pamela Courson.

The Doors were playing on the sound system. I described my three Doors concerts to them. Harvey had only seen the Doors once: in Southern California at the Forum in 1968. He had interviewed the three surviving members and worked with them in the recording studio, music clubs and theater.

Harvey volunteered, "If I ever do a book about the Doors, you should write the introduction."

"Of course!"

I love them madly. I hope you do as well.

Carol Schofield,
MsMusic Productions,
Templeton, California.

Prologue

A month doesn't go by where I'm not asked about the Doors.

This has been going on for 50 years.

I first heard them at Fairfax High School in West Hollywood on Burbank-based AM radio station KBLA, on deejay Dave Diamond's *Diamond Mine* shift. He constantly spun the acetate of their debut long-player in December 1966.

The erudite radio broadcaster explained weekly the origin of their name from the title of a book by Aldous Huxley, *The Doors of Perception*, derived from a line in William Blake's *The Marriage of Heaven and Hell*.

I loved when Diamond segued from "Soul Kitchen" to "Twentieth Century Fox." Some of it sounded like the music they had on KGFJ-AM, my R&B channel, and KBCA-FM, the jazz station. "Break On Through (To the Other Side)" reminded me of Ray Charles's "What'd I Say," from the 1963 Kenny Burrell and Jimmy Smith jazz-arrangement recording of his tune on the Verve label.

I purchased *The Doors* in monaural on the Elektra label that January of 1967 at The Frigate record shop on Crescent Heights and Third Street. I had no idea as a teenager that The Frigate was literally right near the Maharishi Mahesh Yogi–founded Third Street Meditation Center, where Ray Manzarek initially met John Densmore and Robby Krieger in 1965, soon introducing the duo to his buddy Jim Morrison.

In very late 1965 I was at my friend David Wolfe's house on Selmarine Drive in Culver City when the Doors appeared on the 90-minute 10:00 p.m. talk television *The Joe Pyne Show* on KTTV channel 11. We both seem to remember the confrontational host in a heated dialogue with Morrison in Pyne's Beef Box.

I then saw the Doors in January 1967 on the Casey Kasem–hosted afternoon television show *Shebang!* In July I caught the Doors on Dick Clark's *American Bandstand*. I danced occasionally on both Hollywood-based programs between 1965 and 1967.

On April 9, 1967, my cousin Sheila Kubernick telephoned me very late at night. She had just returned from the Cheetah Club in Venice and witnessed the Doors in person. Sheila, a Cher look-alike at the time, was still in a trance, courtesy of Morrison. Sheila later drove my brother Kenny and me to the Valley Music Center for a concert by the Seeds, still reminiscing about the Doors.

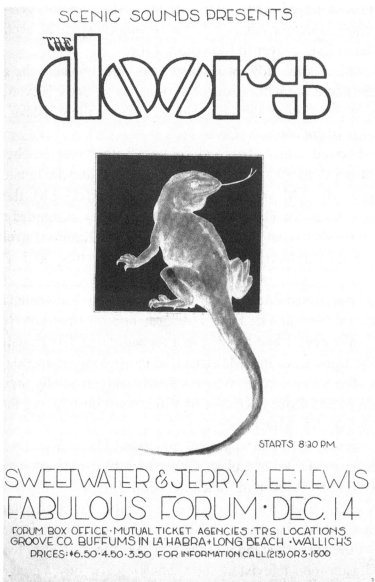

Promotional Handbill courtesy Kirk Silsbee

I went to the Doors concert at the Forum in Inglewood, California, on December 14, 1968. On the show were Jerry Lee Lewis, Sweetwater, and Tzon Yen Luie, who performed with a Chinese stringed instrument, the pipa. I am still recovering from that rendition of "Celebration of the Lizard" and the Doors performing with a string and brass section.

In 1973, I coordinated two accredited upper-division English and music curriculum courses conducted by Dr. James L. Wheeler, assistant professor in the School of Literature at California State University, San Diego. A story in the April 14, 1973, issue of *Billboard* magazine hailed the department's academic aim as "the world's first university level rock studies program."

I placed Jim Morrison's *The Lords and the New Creatures* on the required book list. Manzarek heard about our classes and was very complimentary about students seriously studying Jim as a poet, along with the musical works of Jimi Hendrix, Bob Dylan, the Rolling Stones, Jefferson Airplane, the Beatles, Neil Young, and the Doors. One evening, Ray and trusted associate Danny Sugerman made arrangements for me to screen the existing print of Morrison's *Feast of Friends* movie on campus.

I met Ray in 1974 and interviewed him at Mercury Records on Hollywood Boulevard. I must have interviewed Manzarek a couple of dozen times over 40 years.

I later stumbled across Jim Morrison's grieving partner, Pamela Courson, in April 1974 at a record label party at Danny Sugerman's Laurel Canyon home.

In 1978 Danny Sugerman was a guest on my television program *50/50*, broadcast on Z Channel, public access and Manhattan cable, promoting his just-published book with Jerry Hopkins, *No One Here Gets Out Alive*, the first biography of Jim Morrison. Our half-hour interview was utilized as a prototype Electronic Press Kit by Warner Books advancing Sugerman's book tour.

Record producer Michael Lloyd, musician/songwriter Todd Rundgren and deejay Murray the K were guests on other episodes. I unearthed from Murray's archives a video copy of the Doors'

"People Are Strange" from his *Murray the K in New York* 1967 TV series and aired it.

All during the '80s, Manzarek played piano and organ on a few albums I produced and spoken-word and keyboard collaborations I presented in Santa Monica at McCabe's Guitar Shop with Michael C Ford, Michael McClure and Allen Ginsberg. He lauded my literary work and productions in Westwood on the grounds of UCLA at the Cooperage, Kerckhoff Coffee House and Schoenberg Hall.

In 1990 I served as the project coordinator of *The Jack Kerouac Box* set and invited Manzarek, Allen Ginsberg, Jerry Garcia, Michael C Ford and Michael McClure to contribute to the package booklet liner notes.

In July 1995 in Los Angeles at the MET Theatre on Oxford Avenue I produced and co-curated with director Darrell Larson a month-long *Rock and Roll in Literature* series at the venue. Manzarek, Densmore and Krieger reunited and played "Peace Frog," "Love Me Two Times" and "Little Red Rooster" on July 8. Kirk Silsbee read from Art Pepper's *Straight Life*, John Densmore did an entry from his new novel, and Michael Ontkean recited *Ode to L.A.* by Jim Morrison.

Densmore, on another night, with Paul Lacques, Barbara Williams, Billy Mernit and Andy Krikun performed the work of Bob Dylan with selections from *The Basement Tapes* and *Tarantula*.

Mick Farren, Don Waller, Tim Curry, David Ritz, Roger Steffens, Lewis MacAdams, David Leaf, Bill Pullman, Paul Body, Ed Harris, MET event associate producer Daniel Weizmann and I also shared reflections during July 1995 on Elvis Presley, the Beatles, Bob Marley, Motown and The Band.

During 1996 I produced Ray's double CD audio biography, *The Doors: Myth and Reality—The Spoken Word History*. I'm also cited in the dedication page of Ray's autobiography, *Light My Fire: My Life with the Doors*.

In addition, Manzarek penned the introduction to my 2009 coffee table book, *Canyon of Dreams: The Magic and the Music of Laurel Canyon.* He graciously joined me for California book-signing events in Oakland and San Francisco.

In 2011, Ray, Doors engineer/producer Bruce Botnick, Elliott Lefko of the AEG/Golden Voice company and I took part in a featured panel discussion in the second annual Pollstar Live! Conference, *The Doors—An L.A. Legacy,* held at the Marriott Hotel at L.A. Live in downtown Los Angeles..

In early 2013 Ray emailed me comments for a book my brother Kenneth and I did with photographer Guy Webster, *BIG SHOTS: Rock Legends and Hollywood Icons.* Guy took the photos of *The Doors* LP. John and Robby also provided memories to our Webster text.

My 2014 book *Turn Up the Radio! Rock, Pop and Roll in Los Angeles 1956–1972* is dedicated to Manzarek.

Over the decades I conducted multiple interviews with Manzarek, Densmore and Krieger, who were always accessible and generous with their time and responses. I also interviewed Bruce Botnick, Jac Holzman and Paul A. Rothchild.

As my '60s record album collection grew, it was Ray who turned me on to Bobby Timmons, McCoy Tyner and John Coltrane. John pointed me to Elvin Jones, Chico Hamilton and Fred Katz; Robby alerted me to the Paul Butterfield Blues Band; Bruce engineered and helmed albums by Love; and Jac brought me many vinyl pleasures from his monumental Elektra label.

Jim Morrison made me check out William Blake, Jack Kerouac, Allen Ginsberg, Michael McClure, Lawrence Ferlinghetti, Anaïs Nin, Aldous Huxley and foreign films with subtitles advertised at the single-screen Toho La Brea Theatre.

I had a wonderful lunch and guidance-counselor session with multi-instrumentalist Chris Darrow in 1996 at Ray Manzarek's house in Beverly Hills. Ray dug the Kaleidoscope, a band Chris co-founded, and Chris liked the Doors, whom he caught in 1966 at the Whisky a Go Go.

Chris suggested, "Consider being a bandleader like Duke Ellington." And Ray added, "Yeah, man. Be like the arranger Billy Strayhorn."

Darrow further mandated, "You're gonna have an audience one day that reads your books. It's like building a repertoire. Sometimes it takes 20 years to get the specific charts you want played, recorded and eventually heard."

And so I've decided to be the bandleader and arranger.

A few years ago I began researching, writing and assembling a book on the Doors. I was encouraged by many friends and fans of the Doors who were reading articles I had written in now-defunct magazines and periodicals over the years that were now circulating on the internet.

Summer's Gone is a compilation of raw-transcript interviews with Doors principals Ray, John and Robby, my 1974–2018 reviews of the band's catalog product, and stories, some published and many never in print or online, and requested reflections over five decades, from intimate Doors insiders, poets, writers, musicians, engineers, songwriters, authors, screenwriters, filmmakers and photographers. I imagine this book could be a necessary resource for future biographers.

On January 28, 2018, I attended the memorial tribute and service to Rabbi Isaiah "Shy" Zeldin at the Stephen Wise Temple in the Bel-Air neighborhood of Southern California. Rabbi Eli Herscher praised Zeldin's spiritual and visionary leadership in 1964 as he established an open-minded religious and musical community in the region, a mile from the UCLA campus where Manzarek and Morrison were then enrolled as students. From the Bima, Herscher politely encouraged the congregation of mourners "that today, memory is the only agenda."

This directive applies to our shared experiences with the Doors in these pages.

The Rock and Roll Hall of Fame's Library & Archives on July 10, 2017, invited me to be a guest speaker in their Author Series in Cleveland, Ohio. Before my appearance, one of the curatorial assistants took me into the private air-conditioned storage locker room not open to the viewing public. "We knew you were coming today and pulled out some specific items we wanted you to see."

I was given an envelope containing Jim Morrison's UCLA diploma. It was a signal. I was the showrunner and had been handed the baton at Drake Stadium to finish this 440-yard relay race multi-voice narrative mission.

I initially aimed for a 2016 book publication date that was moved to the 2017 schedule. As I was preparing the manuscript and acquiring photos, it was announced that the Doors were planning a slew of 50th-anniversary products and publicity campaigns during 2017.

Instead of capitalizing on this landmark milestone, publisher Travis Pike made the wise decision to let them take this well-deserved team retail victory lap, and our book would be scheduled for February 12, 2018, Ray Manzarek's birthday.

Then just as we were going to press, in December 2017, we got the news that *The Doors: Live at the Isle of Wight 1970* DVD, their last concert performance ever filmed, was shipping on February 23, 2018.

It was jazz pianist, composer, community activist and bandleader Horace Tapscott, who formed the Pan Afrikan Peoples Arkestra in 1961, who mentioned to me in 1992 at the California African American Museum that "we are not in competition but in collaboration."

I'm from a world of respecting my elders and certainly wasn't gonna jump in front of this long-awaited filmic summary of the Doors' career. And on February 26, my birthday, the time of hesitation is finally through, and you can discover this trip as the first flash of March is upon us.

Harvey Kubernik
February 28, 2018
Los Angeles, California

the doors
summer's gone

by Harvey Kubernik

Steven Van Zandt 2015

I didn't like the Doors as a kid. I didn't get it. I was a total Anglophile on top of being prejudiced against most things from the West Coast. Any guitar player not from the Eric Clapton school was irrelevant, Mike Bloomfield being the only exception, so I didn't appreciate Robby Krieger's Ravi Shankar–influenced guitar style.

Poetry was beyond me, the only exception being Bob Dylan, so Jim Morrison's Rimbaud-meets-Dionysius routine went right over my head.

John Densmore's drumcraft, gently weaving the guitar and keys together, was too subtle in my world of Keith Moon, Ginger Baker and B.J. Wilson.

Ray Manzarek was the exception, being obviously impressive, with every keyboard player tested by his "Light My Fire" riff. But I wouldn't appreciate keyboardists playing with one hand until much later (he played bass with the left).

Nobody in my neighborhood took the band seriously. And while we're on the subject, we let the Rascals get away it, but we weren't so forgiving with the Doors' weird-ass no-bass-thing either.

As it turned out, of course, I couldn't have been more wrong. It's obvious to me now they were fantastic. They would be one of the defining bands of the psychedelic era.

They were a brilliant combination of extremely cinematic rock, pop and art that featured existential philosophy, beat-poet-influenced lyrics, Eastern-style Indian scales, Western-style self-psychoanaylsis and Native American primal, ritual performance.

Awesomely original, they were an unpredictable, exciting, visionary energy for a new world that never quite came to be.

Guy Webster Interview, 2012
Treats! magazine

Q: Your iconic cover photo on the debut Doors album that primarily portrayed Jim Morrison. An LP jacket that brought so many eyes and ears into the brave new mono and stereo world. How did this job happen?

A: Jac Holzman, who owned Elektra Records, called me on the telephone and said, "I have a group I want you to photograph." "OK." "Well, they are out at the Whisky a Go Go." "All right. I'll listen to them." I didn't know who they were. I saw them and I liked them, but I was listening to a lot of stuff back in those days. So we had them scheduled to come into my studio, which at that time was located at my parents' house, in the back. Because even though I was shooting all outdoors stuff at the time, when I wanted to shoot studio, I had a small studio there. And I wanted to do them in the studio so I could get some very intimate pictures of them.

And in walked Jim Morrison. And he said, "Guy." "How do you know me?" "Guy, we went to school together."

"Oh my God. Jim!" We were at UCLA together in the philosophy department, and we used to read Nietzsche together. And I went, "Shit. I didn't know you were a singer or a poet." I was shocked.

And the other guys, and this is a terrible thing, and I know they were angry at me, because I put Jim's face forward and I designed the cover and put the other three guys as his eyes and part of his brain. But I made Jim the star on purpose 'cause I knew it could sell the album. Jac liked it and put that on the cover. He always let me do what I wanted for the cover.

Here's the deal on Jim taking his shirt off for the session. Once we realized that we were in school together and that I was already famous with my album covers, I said, "Look, Jim. You're wearing this shirt and it's embarrassing because it has ribbons on it. I know it's a hippie shirt, but you can buy it in Venice Beach and you can buy it anywhere." And it would have dated him. "I'm gonna take your shirt off. You'll be all right. Trust me. And I'm gonna make you look like Jesus Christ." And that's what it was. And they went with it.

I loved the band live. Oh my God. I later knew that Jim was singing and he had been in class with me. But I was listening to Ray Manzarek's organ. That was brilliant, and that's what impressed me more than anything. Man, this guy could smoke that keyboard, and he was a white guy with little glasses. So I was really impressed.

Q: What about the montage or the superimposition aspect of that first Doors front cover? That was a new thing you were doing.

A: Yes, it was. Because I grew up with jazz and blues and all the album covers were just awful. They were against a yellow background, everybody in suits and similar poses, corny. Except for the work of photographer William Claxton, whom I was friends with, and he shot some great pictures and covers. Good guy and a good artist.

I wanted to do the same with rock 'n' roll. What I wanted was, let's get down to it. Here are these guys, they are singing about love, peace and sex, and I wanted something to make them look sexy and I didn't want them in a studio. I wanted them outdoors in nature, part of our life in the '60s, love-ins, things like that. All natural. And I started putting the musicians and artists outdoors.

But I never thought of Jim as a great singer. He had the emotion. He got into it. I met every great singer years before I heard the Doors. Frank Sinatra, Dean Martin. Jim could get the emotion across and convey everything. Absolutely. He had the ability to tap into the meaning of things he was singing. I thought he was brilliant. But remember—there were a lot of

3

detractors, you know. Everyone didn't like the Doors initially. There was a split group in L.A. But I loved them.

When their album came out, a lot of people I knew never mentioned the band or the album cover. Most of my friends were really square, particularly the show business people. They hadn't really caught on to rock 'n' roll yet. They weren't involved.

Then all of a sudden it exploded. Radio airplay, television shows, magazine stories and their billboard of the first album overlooking Sunset Boulevard. I had an earlier billboard on the Sunset Strip of the Byrds' *Turn! Turn! Turn!* album cover. I knew it was taking rock 'n' roll photography into a new world.

To see something I shot of the Byrds, and then the Doors, in my parents' house and then huge on display on Sunset Strip—I was awestruck by it. It was like, 'Shit... I've made it.' I was doing all right financially, but this was a real assessment of where my career was. I was the first one to have that.

Q: You subsequently were around the Doors for a photo session in Westwood at the Veterans' Cemetery next to UCLA in 1968, when the band did their video for "The Unknown Soldier," from the album *Waiting for the Sun.*

A: Once the Doors hit it big, we really didn't do a whole lot of talking or communicating. We'd go out on location and get it done. I shot the back cover photo on a hill where I did silhouettes of them for their *Waiting for the Sun* album. That was fun.

And the 1968 session around "Unknown Soldier" at the Westwood cemetery. By then Jim had changed. He didn't look as healthy, and his hair was groomed properly. I didn't really look at the photo of Jim in the cemetery again until after he died. I realized it was kind of a requiem for Jim himself.

4

It was raining and very hard to take pictures without getting ugly buildings in the background. The one image on my website has Jim on the side. I was worried about putting it out there because it was too macabre, so I didn't push that photo. I loved the Vietnam commentary being done in front of me. Anything that was political. Morrison had a sense of fashion. He understood. He was super educated, even though he educated himself, going to UCLA at that time in the early '60s, and he came from a junior college.

Q:	You also had an encounter with Jim in 1971.

A:	I was taking pictures of Natalie Wood. She was like a friend of ours, because my first wife and I were very close to Natalie and her husband, Richard Gregson. And I was friends with her. And she said, "Will you do some pictures for me?" "Absolutely."

So we went up to Malibu, to Serra Retreat, and we were shooting there. Not too many cars, and she wouldn't be bothered. And this limousine pulled up and the window came down. And this burly 250-pound man with a full beard and hair said, "Guy." "Who is it?" "Jim." "Jim Morrison?" I didn't recognize him. He asked, "What are you doing?" "Well, I'm just finishing up some work and then I'm moving to Spain and I'll be there for quite a while." And he said he was moving to France in the next week." And I said, "Well, shit, we gotta get in touch." And that was the last time I saw him… I moved to Spain and he moved to France and he died a few months later.

Dr. James Cushing, 2017

It's sometime in 1995, and I'm hosting a Saturday night / Sunday morning mixed-bag eclectic music program called *Toward the One* on San Luis Obispo's otherwise rigidly formatted NPR station. I'm running with a Richard "Groove"

Holmes organ-guitar-drums arrangement of "Song to My Father" and trying to think up the perfect segue when, in an intuitive flash, it comes to me: cue up "You're Lost Little Girl" from *Strange Days* and see what happens. No, John Densmore's beat doesn't swing the way the Holmes track swings, and Robby Krieger's beautiful guitar filigrees are more about flamenco than gutbucket. And yet—the tempo's similar, the Ray Manzarek organ registration's sweetly close, and there's something intangibly… I dunno… recognizable there, some similarity that seems for that midnight moment so obviously right…

And today, as I notice that 50 blessed years have somehow passed since the Doors' first Elektra recording sessions, I look back at that moment and wonder: Was I only imagining that connection, maybe wishing it into being? Or, is one part of the Doors' lasting power their music's tantalizing proximity to the organ-guitar-drums "soul jazz" that swept the nation between 1956 and '66?

We all know there were secrets to the Doors. One of them was that a poet, a real poet in the visionary tradition of Percy Shelley and Arthur Rimbaud, lived behind the hunky lead singer's perfect face.

What is it about the Doors that we still talk about and love their music? The answer is, if there were an answer to that question, we would all know it. We are trying to define the mystery of art and the essence of the mystery of art is its resistance to definition. The Doors set something into motion in the air, and it comes into people's minds and heads through their ears and something else is set into motion. And that's just about the most accurate description I can make.

Thinking about the Doors. There is something in their music that is always pointing towards something else that is evoked but never named. Whether it's theater or poetry or jazz or the darkly complex sexual desires or the sense of the ongoing presence of the Native American nations or the sense that one somehow is living in a world in which one's parents had been always dead and buried even before you were alive.

The Doors evoked this in a way that no other rock band ever has. And I don't how they do that. I don't know if anyone else needs too. But it makes their accomplishment unique, and whenever I listen to the Doors I am never aware that I am listening to music from the '60s or from any other period. I feel like I'm listening to something that is contemporary. And the same is true with Jimmy Smith and Miles Davis of the same period.

So the Doors always had a jazz influence, and in the almost 50 years since they ended, the jazz influence has swallowed them in the sense that they are a jazz group now. In the same way that the young Bob Dylan was influenced by Woody Guthrie and now he is Woody Guthrie.

Eddi Fiegel, 2017

I first discovered the Doors in my early teens during the 1980s, and despite the fact that in London, at least, they were far from cool at that time, my fascination soon turned into a minor obsession.

My best friend Lisa and I would spend hours pressing the pause and rewind buttons on our parents' VHS players watching film clips of the group's TV performances and interviews with Jim Morrison.

Having read about the band and where their name had come from, I was eager to get to the source, as it were, and find out just what Jim had found so fascinating about Aldous Huxley's *Doors of Perception*. This I did, and I was equally enthralled. So much so that when it came to games lessons at my girls' high school, an hour with my book seemed much more appealing.

As a not particularly athletic 14-year-old, I found less than attractive the idea of standing around on a netball court in the chilly British winter wearing a ridiculously short, pleated miniskirt whilst pretending to be enthusiastic about throwing a ball into a basket on a pole. So, hoping I wouldn't be spotted between the hanging duffle coats, I had settled down in the relative warmth of the cloakroom, cocooned with my Penguin paperback of Huxley's essay.

Leaving behind the North-West London suburbia outside the school door, I could sit around with Native American Indians discovering this technicolor world of mescaline and peyote experimentation, knowing that somewhere along the line, this very text had inspired the music I adored.

"*What* are you doing?" bellowed Miss Chalcott, the stridently built PE teacher, as she stormed in discovering my hideout. *The Doors of Perception* was not on the list of recommended reads supplied by the school, and even if it had been, I suspect I would still have received the detention which Miss Chalcott lost no time in dishing out.

A few years later, I rushed off to a London record store when I heard that John Densmore was going to be signing copies of his new autobiography. Nerves twisting my stomach, I told him how I had spent years in my bedroom wearing out my Doors albums playing them over and over again. "Well, I'm glad you came out of that bedroom."

Decades on, the Doors are hip once more. My perspective may be different now, but listening to those records still transports me to some other world where the sun shines by day and the moon gleams by night and whatever time it may be, something mesmerizing seems just around the corner.

David N. Pepperell, 2017

From the moment we heard Ray Manzarek's whirling dervish calliope organ and Jim's opening statement powering out of our radios, Australia fell in love with the Doors.

"Light My Fire" was all over the airwaves, Jim's face adorned the front cover of numerous, and not just music, magazines, and the first, eponymous album was being played and discussed all around the country. Here, out of the vortex that the late '60s were, was a new sound, a new message and a shamanic call in their record "Break On Through."

I can recall no other album that inspired listeners in this country so much as 1967's *The Doors*. Its bleak darkness and strange invocations seemed to point to a new direction, not so much peace and love as blood and fire. We were trying to understand the revolutionary rock of American bands— like the Grateful Dead, Jefferson Airplane and Quicksilver Messenger Service—and the Doors, far more so than those groups, seemed to sketch out a path to the future.

Mostly self-composed, with a couple of tunes by Weill and Wolf, the album's songs bristled with energy and ecstasy. "Soul Kitchen," "Break On Through" and "Take It as It Comes" were declamatory orations balanced by cool reflections like "The Crystal Ship," "I Looked at You" and "End of the Night," followed by the climactic Oedipal horror show of "The End," a strange choice to close a debut album but an aural experience that was totally new to us.

This was bigger than pop music, perhaps the beginning of what was to be called rock music, and was obviously meant to be listened to closely, not just to be used as a background for dancing. "Light My Fire" was the catalyst to their breakthrough, changing them from a literary, existential musical force to a teenage sensation and making Jim Morrison a rock 'n' roll icon right from the beginning.

Sadly, the Doors never played Australia, so we never had the great good fortune to see them perform their music onstage, but we had the concert films and the *Absolutely Live* LP to give us some idea of what that would be like. Not as good as the real thing, of course, but those mediums did let us see that the Doors were so much more than a musical group but a major cultural force that would have huge impact on not only the U.S. but the whole world.

We bought all the classic ensuing albums, embraced the later hit singles and then cried when Jim died, far too young, at the dawning of a new decade, as if only the majesty of the '60s could contain him.

Seven albums in five years, all of them of a wonderful nature and of the highest quality, is one hell of an effort!

Even their *Absolutely Live* album, usually an excuse for a greatest hits compilation, contained the only recorded version of their greatest theatrical tour de force, "The Celebration of the Lizard."

The Doors are still one of the most played groups on Australian radio and sell albums by the thousands here every year. Add to that the fact our local group The Australian Doors Show played for seven years, did 1,200 shows all over the world and was regarded as the best Doors cover band in the world in their time, and you can see how much Australia loved the Doors and always will.

Jesus, we wish they had come out here and played for us.

Peter Lewis, 2017

Today is my birthday. I'm 72. I played a gig last night with my daughter. Anyway, I was talking to a friend who came to see us about "getting older." I don't know how the subject of dreams came up. But we had a puff in his car after the gig, and he had said something about waking up with his heart pounding some nights ago.

We had been talking about a story I'm writing. My theory is that death isn't waiting for us down the road somewhere. What this might be in real terms is debatable. But I believe it is the sum of all our past collective memories trying to project themselves into the future.

In our waking lives we can stay in front of these, trying to keep history from repeating itself. But in our dream life, there is no way to keep them out of our consciousness. In dreams we share responsibility for the preconception we have of each other.

My friend, who is 20 years younger than me, was talking about how he had learned to control his dreams. My response was: "Then why would you wake up with your heart pounding the other night?" He just looked at me the way people do sometimes when they get interrupted. Anyway, I told him not to worry. It just meant he was getting older. But I felt him getting paranoid.

So I told him I had gotten these ideas from Jim Morrison.

Before they got famous, the Doors had come in for an audition at Gazzarri's on the Strip. This would have been '65 or '66, when I was playing there in Peter and the Wolves, trading sets with Pat and Lolly Vegas. It was a Sunday afternoon as I sat there with Pat Vegas and Bill Gazzarri watching.

None of us had seen anything like this before. Jim stalking the stage and growling over the mic was all it took to freak Bill out. So the Doors didn't get the gig on the Strip.

But when another less conservative Gazzarri's opened down on La Cienega, the Doors became the house band.

In the meantime I had gotten in Moby Grape. The Tropicana Motel on Santa Monica Boulevard next to Barney's Beanery, where all the rock groups stayed in L.A. Jim was wandering around out by the pool when I ran into him. We ended up talking in his room for a couple of hours.

I left with a sense of him having revealed to me a great truth about life and death. It would take years to figure this out

11

the way I described it to my friend. But I always remembered the heart of Jim's message was about music and how using it as a vehicle to keep life in front of you and death behind is a good example.

Anyway, my friend liked the Doors. So he lightened up on me when I told him, "When you get older and lose control of your dreams, it's just death catching up to you. But don't worry, man. It's all right. Just don't let it catch you looking backwards."

Ram Dass, 1999

My favorite album psychedelic experiences were with *Sgt. Pepper's*, early Bob Dylan, and Miles Davis's *Sketches of Spain*. That music would take me out. I loved the Doors. Sure. "Light My Fire," of course. Some Eastern influences in their music.

Jim Morrison was a poet... I liked the level of reality he played with. I like people pushing the edge and getting out of the linearity. I love that. And not in a kind of clever, studied way, but in an ecstatic experiential way. That's what I love better. That's what he tried to do.

Roger Steffens, 2017

In early November 1967, I was a recent draftee passing through Berkeley, and after seeing Janis Joplin and Ike & Tina Turner at Winterland, I was off to Vietnam. I landed in Saigon, and within three weeks I realized the whole dismal affair was a fraud, corrupt from top to bottom, just a way to make money off young kids' lives.

One of our only ointments against the depravities was music. This was the time of an impressive increase in headphone advertising, and listeners were discovering this new audio stereo world. Exposure and sales made a difference. So one of the most popular areas of the Vietnam PXs was their music section. The PX sold a variety of Japanese headphones. Everyone wanted them. Stereo was really coming into its own at that point.

During the entire 26 months I was in Vietnam, a poet friend, Jerry Burns, who had published my first two poetry anthologies, taped eight hours of KSAN-FM every week. It had quickly morphed from KMPX into the quintessential FM underground radio station in the San Francisco Bay Area. You could hear it as you walked the streets of Berkeley in the summertime and not even need a radio because KSAN blared from every open window and park bench. Jimi Hendrix, Van Morrison, the Grateful Dead, Jefferson Airplane, Moby Grape, Quicksilver Messenger Service and, of course, the Doors.

Jerry sent four-track reel-to-reel eight-hour tapes from the Oakland Army Base every Monday afternoon and I would then dub cassettes off my big TEAC reel-to-reel. I made hundreds of cassettes to give to guys out in the field and they, in turn, would copy them and circulate them among their buddies.

So we had a very up-to-the-minute soundtrack to Vietnam, thanks especially to Scoop Nisker's phenomenal stream-of-consciousness sound-collage newscasts that told us what was really going on back in the world from a very left-centered perspective. And guys got tapes from home. In the barracks we all had stereo systems: TEAC or Akai tape recorders, a Kenmore or Macintosh amp. Fisher Stereo, Toshiba. Those companies all had local offices. Gorgeous girls in miniskirts at the PXs were selling sports cars with life insurance attached. If you didn't make it through the war, your family or your girlfriend would still get your car. What did you have to spend money on? You were housed and fed.

13

There was also Jimi Hendrix's *Are You Experienced.* On May 12 it was released on the Reprise label. Jimi and the Doors were popular in the barracks. Hendrix opened an aural door that I didn't know existed before. (I wrote a whole chapter about the quintessential importance of Jimi for us, trapped there in the midst of an unjust war, called *Nine Meditations on Jimi and Nam*, assigned as part of a major coffee table book, *The Ultimate Hendrix.*)

I heard the debut Doors album in January 1967, *Strange Days* and in 1968, *Waiting for the Sun.* You can only imagine how much "Unknown Soldier" resonated with me. I loved "Touch Me" on *The Soft Parade.* Morrison's poetry got to me the same way I was later attracted to the poetry of Bob Marley. I liked Jim's wildness. The revelation aspect. We played Doors music a lot in Vietnam.

In 1967 I hardly saw any marijuana around America. And when I went to Vietnam, maybe 10 percent of the soldiers smoked, although it was available on any street corner in Saigon. But within two years, I'd say 70 percent of everybody, up to and including lieutenants and captains, smoked. My apartment became a safe haven for soldiers in their off-duty hours to share a spliff away from the shatter of bombs and mortars.

Saigon Sally was a Vietnamese woman who rode on the back of a motorcycle with her boyfriend looking for GIs sitting in sidewalk cafés at whom she could toss grenades. What I'm saying in effect is that there were no front lines in Vietnam. There were some kick-ass battles, but then the enemy would go back down their tunnels or caves in the mountains where they were hiding. You could lose your life anywhere at any time, on the street or in the boonies. That put a 24/7 strain on you psychologically, and you needed something to cut that.

For most of the older guys, the lifers, there was alcohol. If you are drunk and suddenly come under attack, you're still gonna be blind drunk. But if you're stoned, I found, you could straighten out very quickly from the adrenaline. And I certainly needed something to cut the tension.

So I taught myself how to smoke pot in order to do that. It leveled things out and enhanced what was going on. You were in a totally foreign environment, even the air was different. It was yellow and tactile. And you knew the other off-duty soldiers were just as hazy as you were.

I can't begin to tell you how terrific it was to hear Phil Ochs, the Doors, the Mamas and the Papas, Donovan singing "The War Drags On." Creedence Clearwater Revival's "Run Through the Jungle," "Fortunate Son" and "Who'll Stop the Rain." Buffalo Springfield. Dr. John. Crosby, Stills and Nash's soothing-the-nerves debut LP.

As for the Doors and Vietnam, the placement of "The End" in *Apocalypse Now* was essential. They've had other songs in Vietnam-themed movies like *Gardens of Stone*.

"Light My Fire" was such a great anthem; I could never get enough of the long version. In fact, on my first, pure Sandoz acid trip I heard that song. We had dropped on the sunrise shores of Lake Michigan where poet friends and I stared at scores of Vietnamese peasants in conical straw hats planting rice in the lake. It was a never-to-be-forgotten mass hallucination.

To me Jim Morrison was marketed as a kind of young Dylan Thomas–Lord Byron character, a claim that is not without its validity. But I think it probably drove him crazy, from what his friends have told me. He wanted to finally grow out of that. It's like John Lennon taking his naked pictures.

I have a theory, and it's been proven to me from the reception and media coverage of my Instagram, *The Family Acid*. And it applies to bands like the Doors. There's a tremendous interest now among the tech generation for true imagery from a time that now is being transformed into mythology. For analog versus digital. Unless you lived through the Psychedelic Revolution, you can't fully overstand that experience.

I attach specific dates to most of the slides that we post, which leads to our followers making comments like, "OMG, this is the month or the week or the day I was born," wishing they had arrived earlier to feel The Vibes.

I think about the great artists who didn't make it out alive, tragic lessons for us all. After my discharge I spent all of 1970 speaking out nationally against the war.

At the end of that year, utterly disillusioned, I left America and ended up for most of 1971 in Marrakech. I had a letter of introduction to a French countess who had a massive palace in the European section of that venerable city. Her young son Jean was about to turn 21 and inherit the title of his late father, the Count de Breteuil. He showed up in town on a Sunday evening. My wife and I were invited the next day to dinner at the Villa Taylor. There, Jean and his girlfriend, Marianne Faithfull, told us a story about discovering Jim Morrison's body in a bathtub in the Marais in Paris the previous Saturday.

For days there was no news anywhere, and we began to doubt his tale. How could someone so famous die and nobody know? Eventually the story broke and was an enormous sensation.

Back in the mid-'80s I was hosting an NPR show called *The Sound of the Sixties* and had John Densmore on as a guest, and I told him that story. He told me he had been hearing rumors for years but knew nothing of the circumstances, and asked me if he could use the transcript of our talk for his book, *Riders on the Storm*.

When it was published, the ghoulish Albert Goldman called me and said I had the key to what everyone was looking for, and said he'd even been to the morgue where Jim's body was briefly held, asking if he could fly out to California to interview me. I refused to speak with him again, and he died shortly after. For me, hearing about Jim's death was just terribly sad.

Ray Manzarek - Harvey Kubernik Interviews (1974-2013) in *Melody Maker, Goldmine, HITS, MOJO, THC Expose, RecordCollectorNews.com* and *CaveHollywood.com.*

Raymond Daniel Manzarek (born Raymond Daniel Manczarek) was born in Chicago. Ray resided with his family n the south side of Chicago and graduated from DePaul University with a B.A. degree in economics.

In the early 1960s the Manzarek clan relocated to the South Bay Redondo Beach community in Southern California.

It was in Westwood, California, in the campus of UCLA in 1964–65 that keyboardist Manzarek first met writer James Douglas Morrison, a transfer student from Florida State University. At the UCLA Film School, Ray earned a master's degree in cinematography and Jim a B.S. degree in the theater arts department of the College of Fine Arts.

While performing with Ray and the Ravens in the summer of 1965, Manzarek saw Morrison again at Venice Beach, and they discussed forming a band together.

In 1965 Ray was introduced to Richard Bock, owner of the monumental World Pacific Records. The label was home to Chet Baker, Les McCann, Barney Kessel, Shelley Manne, Shorty Rogers, Jim Hall, Don Ellis, Joe Pass, Gerry Mulligan, Russ Freeman, Art Pepper and Ravi Shankar. Bock introduced the practice of Transcendental Meditation to Manzarek and gave him two LPs by Maharishi Mahesh Yogi.

Rick and the Ravens cut a few promotional singles for World Pacific's Aura Records, the rock subdivision. On March 26, 1965, the group appeared on the Marvin Miller– hosted *Screen Test* on KCOP-TV channel 13 at 10 p.m.

I tuned in for Eddie Cano, April and Nino, Jackie DeShannon and Cannibal and the Headhunters but faintly recall Rick and the Ravens performing "Henrietta." Contestants were paired with celebrities to identify old movie clips—a perfect way for a film student to make some extra money.

Bock further touted mantra meditation and spirituality to Ray, who then steered him to a 30-person class inside the Third Street Meditation Center in Los Angeles, where he encountered two Los Angeles natives: drummer John Densmore and guitarist Robby Krieger.

Densmore, a graduate of University High School, went to Santa Monica City College and San Fernando Valley State College. Krieger, from Pacific Palisades High School, attended UC–Santa Barbara and then UCLA. Densmore and Krieger had briefly been in a group called the Psychedelic Rangers in 1965.

In early September '65, Ray Manzarek, his brothers Jim and Rick, Jim Morrison, John Densmore and a bass player named Patricia Sullivan recorded a demo in lieu of another single session date at Bock's World Pacific studio on Third Street in West Hollywood.

Their acetate results were "Moonlight Drive," "My Eyes Have Seen You," "Summer's Almost Gone," "Hello, I Love You," "End of the Night" and "Go Insane."

In October Ray revamped the Rick and the Ravens lineup, adding Robby Krieger, and along with Morrison and Densmore, they became the Doors.

The determined band members dropped off the acetate to record labels in town: RCA, Capitol, Liberty, Decca, Dunhill and Warner/Reprise all rejected them.

Eventually it caught the attentive ears of Billy James at Columbia Records, where the Doors had a short-lived stay before finding permanent residence at Elektra Records, the home of the brotherhood from 1966 until 1971.

Ray Manzarek at Sunset Sound.
Photo by Henry Diltz

HK: In 1963, you were in the U.S. Army stationed at a Southeast Asia military base in Korat, Thailand.

RM: Everyone had to do military service. This was a time just before Vietnam. I was lucky I was in Fort Ord for basic training. I played with jazz drummer Oliver Johnson. And then I went to Fort Monmoth signal school as a darkroom man, and then they sent me off to Okinawa and then to Thailand.

Besides Thailand, I went to New York City and then I went to Okinawa, fell in with a group of musicians, smoked a little grass there. I thought it was fabulous. Then I went to Thailand, where I had my real first Thai stick experience. Courtesy of Uncle Sam.

The first time I smoked pot was back in Thailand. When I was in the Army we lived in these little Quonset huts. These little shacks. There was an air base that we were connected with. You would have little house boys from the nearby village in Korat who would shine your shoes, take care of your clothes for you, help clean the barracks. You would pay them a couple a bucks a month and they were more than happy. One day, I asked one of the boys, maybe age 12 or 13, "Can you get me ganja?" And the kid just froze for a second. "You smoke ganja?" "Yes. I would like some ganja."

What happened was that earlier I had gotten a joint from one of my black brothers. So I said, "I will trade you cigarettes for marijuana." I exchanged a carton of American cigarettes that cost me around two dollars on the PX base and he brought me some Thai sticks stuffed into a can of Saltine crackers. To him that was like the greatest deal he could have ever imagined. The pot cost him nothing, he cut it off at the bottom of a stalk and put into a foot-long can with a lid on it. Now, he would normally buy one of those cartons from one of the GIs for four dollars. I got it for him at two dollars. And he would take that thing and sell it and make like eight to ten dollars on a carton.

It was a Saturday night. Nothing to do. So we decided to smoke this stuff. I had a couple of hits and came on. The first trip was when I realized what the word *stoned* was. I could not move. I sat there and looked into outer space stoned out of my mind. It wasn't a giggling thing. It was a profound awakening. "Oh my God." And every five minutes I would have to stick my tongue back into my mouth. Little by little. Sort of choking and realizing my tongue was all the way out of my mouth and I had to push it back in. I was sitting there like a moron, stoned and just in a complete state of absolute joy. Not giggly or silly. Just amazed at the profundity of being alive on planet Earth. This went on for four hours while we drank some Cokes and ate pound cake from a nearby snack stand.

Q: You and Jim went to the UCLA film school and were students in the motion picture division. You had a class with the French director Jean Renoir.

A: Jim came from Florida, I came from Chicago. We smoked pot together, we talked philosophy together. We had a class with the German director Josef von Sternberg. This was in 1965. Von Sternberg, the great German director of Marlena Dietrich, who did *The Blue Angel, Morocco* and *Shanghai Express.*

In my student film *Evergreen* I used as music the opening strain of "The Young Rabbits" by the Jazz Crusaders. The best 20 UCLA films by students were shown at Royce Hall to the public. And von Sternberg came up to me after I screened *Evergreen* and said, "Very good, Manzarek. Very good." One of the greatest moments of my life. So he's the guy who really kind of gave a real sense of darkness to the Doors—not that we wouldn't have been there anyway.

But having von Sternberg seeing the deep psychology of his movies, and the pace at which he paced his films, really influenced Doors songs and Doors music. The sheer psychological weight of his movies on what we tried to do with our music.

The film school is always there. Our song structure was based on the cinema. Loud. Soft. Gentle. Violent. A Doors song is, again, aural, and aural cinema. We always tried to make pictures in your mind. Your mind ear. You hear pictures with the music itself.

In 1965 we graduated. Jim got his bachelor's degree, I got my master's degree—and we were hopefully going to do something together. But Jim said he was going to New York City. I thought, "Well, that's it. I'll never see Jim again."

Q: I walked with you on Venice Beach years ago, and you pointed at the sand many years ago and said, "This is where Jim sang the lyrics to 'Moonlight Drive' to me in a Chet Baker–like voice."

A: When I first heard Jim sing in Venice, I thought he had it. Interestingly, on "Moonlight Drive," that is really a seminal, or a signpost song. I thought it was brilliant. His voice had a softness to it. It's the first song Jim Morrison sang to me on the beach. It had been after we graduated UCLA and I ran into him on the beach. "What have you been doing?" "I've been writing songs." "Sing me a song." "I'm shy." "You're not shy. Stop it. There's nobody here. Just you and me. I'm not judging your voice. I just want to hear the song. Besides, you used to sing with Rick and the Ravens at the Turkey Joint West in Santa Monica and did 'Louie Louie' until you could not talk."

Q: I know Jim played tambourine one evening with Rick and the Ravens when you were booked with Sonny & Cher at a high school event, the duo never showed up. Jim said that was the easiest $25 he ever made. And then he went into a garage rehearsal room with the Doors. Was Jim a natural frontman at the Turkey Joint West?

A: No. [Laughs.] It took a while and later to work it out onstage at the London Fog and Whisky a Go Go. But by God, he sure did scream a lot and sure had a willing injection of energy into rock 'n' roll.

Q: Before the Doors inked a Record deal with Jac Holzman and Elektra Records, in December, 1965 the Doors had a six month provisional contract with Columbia Records. Billy James, the former publicist for Columbia, was now the manager of talent acquisition and development for Columbia. The label never assigned a producer or even committed to a recording session.

A: Without Billy James, the Doors would have never made it. Oh my God. I got my Vox Continental courtesy of

Billy James. He had heard the original rough Doors demo and said, "You guys got something. You're going all the way." Jim dropped off the acetate at Columbia.

Billy said, "Welcome to Columbia Records. Is there anything we can do for you guys?" And we said, "Yeah. You can give us some front money. Do we get paid for signing?" "No, we don't do that. Do you need any equipment?"

At the time I was playing my brother Jim's Wurlitzer keyboard. On the demo it was a piano. Columbia had just bought up Vox. Billy offered, "You want a Vox Continental, Ray?" "Yes!" Every English group plays one. The Animals, the Dave Clark 5, Manfred Mann. "Go out to the Vox plant in the San Fernando Valley. It's right across the street from the Budweiser plant."

We jump in John's van and see what we pick up. Robby gets an extra guitar. And we got two amps with 14-inch speakers. We went around to the loading dock and picked up the stuff and got out of there like bandits.

Q: And Billy eventually joined Elektra Records in 1967. Let's discuss your debut LP *The Doors*. It was done at Sunset Sound with producer Paul A. Rothchild and engineer Bruce Botnick.

A: Sunset Sound was a very hip recording studio on Sunset Boulevard. The Beach Boys had been there. Herb Alpert, Love. It was owned by a trumpet player, [Salvador] Tutti Camarata, and he had the Camarata Strings, I believe.

Q: He arranged Billie Holiday's final album—*Lady in Satin*. That room was built by Disney money.

A: Nice money. It was an excellent recording studio, four tracks. Rothchild and Botnick. Never had met engineer Bruce before. Paul was the producer.

Rothchild and Botnick are Door number 5 and Door number 6. There's four Doors in the band and two Doors in the control room. So, they were always there, always twisting the knobs and really on top of it. A couple of high-IQ, very intelligent guys. We couldn't have done it without them.

Paul Rothchild was the guy who had produced the Paul Butterfield Blues Band. And Botnick worked with Love. So, Robby was a big fan of the Butterfield Blues Band and he was very excited that Paul Rothchild was gonna produce for us. I didn't know either one of them and not familiar with their work outside of Love. I had heard Paul Butterfield and thought it was good. Chicago blues by Chicago white boys. Being a Chicago white boy myself, I could identify with Chicago white boys playing the blues. So it was a great combination of six guys.

That first album was basically the four Doors and the two other Doors in the control room making the sound. We made the music. They made the sound. And they did an absolutely brilliant job. And it was a real joy and a great learning experience.

I had been in the World Pacific studio before, but Jim had never been in a vocal booth. He had some hesitations because he was a rookie. Well, the whole thing took 10 days. Boom. We're done. We're out of here. "Light My Fire" was two takes. "The End" was two takes, which was a major ordeal because there were certain substances floating around everyone's brain—to wit, LSD—and to record on LSD was quite difficult. But Morrison thought that would be a good idea for him to sing and do "The End" on LSD. None of the rest of us took acid as we were recording. However, we did indulge in smoking marijuana. And that really started with our second album.

Rothchild and Botnick were two alchemists with sound. We were the alchemical music makers, but they were alchemists with sound—adding a bit of this, a bit of that. Some reverb. Some high end. Let's hit it at 20K or 10K. Let's dial in a bit of bass in there. They were making this evil witch's brew concoction as we went along. And the sound just got better and better.

Q: And on this album, and subsequent sessions, you were joined by a studio bassist who essentially followed and copied your bass lines done on the Fender Rhodes.

A: I was the bass player of the Doors. When it came to recording, I played a Fender Rhodes keyboard bass. The instrument was great in person because it had a deep rich sound and moved a lot of air. But in the recording studio it lacked a pluck. It did not have the attack that a bass guitar would have—especially if you played a bass guitar with a pick. You had plenty of attack. So, on some of the songs we brought in an actual bass player, one of the Los Angeles cats, Larry Knechtel. Who played the same bass line that I played on "Light My Fire," who doubled my bass line. They could then get rid of my bass part and use the nice sound that Larry Knechtel could get. The click and the bottom. Dave Diamond, a deejay [on KBLA] broke "Light My Fire."

Q: The keyboard was treated equally and not an overdub or buried below in the mix.

A: Well, it had to be. We were the Modern Jazz Quartet! It is a collective journey, that's a good way of putting it. It's of course Jim Morrison as the charismatic lead singer, and I've got to address Jim Morrison, but it's Densmore, Krieger and Manzarek [too]. It's a journey of these four guys, the Four Horsemen of the Apocalypse, the diamond-shaped, no-bass-player that made a five-point pentagram, shape of the diamond. It's the inverted pyramid. It's an archetypal journey

25

of four young men into the unconscious, and coming out of that and creating a musical art form.

Q: You then start the *Strange Days* LP.

A: Album two is recorded on an eight-track. The first album was four-track. We now had four more tracks. That meant everything that we could do on the first album, we would still have four more tracks left over for overdubs, for experimentation. So we experimented in and out of the universe.

Q: You saw the studio becoming a laboratory.

A: Exactly. It was a place where we could really experiment. We could put on our lab tech coats rather than coming in with our "mod" outfits. It's almost as if we put on our glasses. I felt like I was in a 1932 German science fiction movie, *Woman in the Moon*, something along that line. Some Fritz Lang. It was like *Metropolis* and we were wearing those glasses that you wear so you don't get sparks in your eyes and we had lab coats on. And we were preparing this strange concoction called *Strange Days*.

Q Jim Morrison's voice really went further and deeper on the *Strange Days* expedition.

A: Well, the man had his chops, as they say. Jim got his chops together. He had a thick bull neck resembling a large engorged male organ. [Laughs.] And by then, he could sing, man. That throat had opened up and that man was singing.

Q: On *Strange Days* your organ work offers a tiny tip of the hat to Herbie Hancock, specifically his composition "Watermelon Man," on "When the Music's Over."

26

A: Oh, absolutely. That's Herbie Hancock, man. I'm borrowing a little bit of Herbie's piano line. My keyboard line is a variation of his piano line on "Watermelon Man." Like Jim would say, "We'll steal from anybody." [Laughs.] "Beggars borrow. Geniuses steal."

Q: As you are hearing Jim's lyrics to "When the Music's Over," late 1967, this is a timeline pre–Earth Day that began in 1970. Those lyrics are detailing ecological concerns and environmental chaos.

A: Sure, absolutely man. But don't forget that's late 1967, and the potheads were aware. That's what was so great about marijuana opening the doors of perception, along, of course, with LSD. Marijuana makes you aware that you are on a planet.
It's God's good green earth and you've got to take care of God's good clean earth. The potheads were the first mass ecological movement. And I hope they continue on and continue it into the future, because it's our obligation to save the planet.

Q: You then already had been enlightened before the Doors really opened.

A: Oh yes. Well, that's what I applied to the music. That was the whole point of it. LSD was around. Jim Morrison had taken LSD. I had taken LSD. It was not illegal then.

Q: How did it impact the music and personal journey?

A: Well, it turns you into God. That's what it does. [Laughs.] You become one with the universe. I read Sigmund Freud's book *Moses and Monotheism* concerning the relationship of Moses and the Egyptian pharaoh Akhenaten.

Freud claims Moses was an übermensch at Akhenaten's court. Akhenaten threw away all the old gods of ancient Egypt and instituted the sun—the Aten—as the sole god. Hence, monotheism. It was like, "Wait a minute. That's the exact same experience I had on the beach in Venice with the sun shining out of the heavens on me."

Q: Why do Jim Morrison's lyrics work so well just on the printed page without any music in back or in front of the words?

A: I knew Jim was a great poet. There's no doubt about that. See, that's why we put the band together in the first place. It was going to be poetry together with rock 'n' roll. Not like poetry and jazz. Or like, it was poetry and jazz from the '50s, except we were doing poetry and rock 'n' roll. And our version of rock 'n' roll was whatever you could bring to the table. Robby, bring your flamenco guitar, Robby, bring that bottleneck guitar, bring that sitar tuning. John, bring your marching drums and your snares and your four on the floor. Ray, bring your classical training and your blues training and your jazz training. Jim, bring your Southern gothic poetry, your Arthur Rimbaud poetry. It all works in rock 'n' roll. So Jim was a magnificent poet. I loved his poetry. The fact that he was doing ecological poetry.

Well, you know, Harvey, because lyrics are poetry. The words were well edited. Jim was good that way when it came to songs. When you are doing this written poetry you can really stretch out and you can really expand. And, no one so far has done an Ezra Pound on Jim Morrison. With his poetry, he'd throw this out, take this line, or two lines, but when it comes to music, you gotta be very choosy, because you only have a short period of time.

Q: Again, in the second Doors album journey, Rothchild and Botnick are taking the whole trip into a new sonic blueprint world.

A: Absolutely. We knew each other. We were friends. We would hang out together. We would get high together and go to each other's houses and hang out.

My God, *Strange Days*, what an album cover. We told the art director from Elektra Records, Bill Harvey, "Make something Fellini-esque." And he did that on his own. That's all we told him. We saw the photos and said, "Bill, this is fabulous. You've outdone yourself." And Bill said, before he died, "That's the best album cover I ever did."

Q: And then the *Waiting for the Sun* disc. Some songs for this album already existed in raw form but a lot of new material was written for this endeavor. You did it at T.T.G. Studios. The Mothers of Invention, Eric Burdon and the Animals, the Velvet Underground with Nico, the Monkees, Linda Ronstadt, Jimi Hendrix, Tommy Vig, Little Feat, and producers Tom Wilson and Kim Fowley used the room.

Kim described T.T.G. to me as "a giant cheeseburger box with high ceilings owned by a sound engineer, an Israeli named Amnon 'Ami' Hadani, who built studios and worked with Tom Wilson and Frank Zappa on *Freak Out* and *Absolutely Free*."

A: You know it's time to do a record when you have 10 or 12 songs together. When it hits a dozen, time to enter the recording studio. I mean, we worked on those songs. I mean, when we would get together in the rehearsal studio, they were polished. They were changed. They were adapted. Somebody, invariably Robby or Jim who would come up with the original idea. But boy, the four of us would get together, change and modify and polish the songs.

29

Q: "Hello, I Love You" from *Waiting for the Sun* had been around for a while.

A: Yes. It was a song Jim wrote on the beach when we used to live down in Venice. Dorothy [Fujikawa], my soon-to-be wife, would go off to work and Jim and I would go off to the beach around the rings on the sand at Muscle Beach and work out around the bars, rings and swings and get ourselves into physical shape. He was gorgeous. Man, he was perfect. He was a guy who had opened the doors of perception and made a blend of the American Indian and the American Cowboy. He was the white Anglo-Saxon Protestant. The WASP who had taken on the mantle of the American Indian. He now was no longer a fighter of Indians. He was a lover of American Indians. Like John F. Kennedy, that guy would have been a great president. Pre-alcohol, would have been a great president. The alcohol unfortunately destroyed Jim Morrison.

Q: Once again, warnings about the environment are inherent in the album.

A: Sure. Yes. Ecology was very, very big. We were all trying to save the planet. The sun was the energy. The supreme energy.

The establishment, as we called it, the squares, as they were called in the '50s, the establishment as they were called in the '60s, were trying to stop drug use, the smoking of marijuana, were trying to stop any kind of organic fertilizer. The word *organic* to them meant hippie, radical potheads and people who wanted to leave behind the organized religions and start some new tribal religion based on American Indian folklore. That's indeed what we were. We called ourselves the new tribe.

Q: You and Dorothy were living in Venice, but the band was based in Laurel Canyon. So was your producer Paul Rothchild.

In 2008 I interviewed producer Rick Rubin for my *Canyon of Dreams: The Magic and the Music of Laurel Canyon* book and he dug Paul.

Rick told me, "I love him. Paul Rothchild's records feel immediate and lively like you're there. He gets out of the way of the performance; you get to feel the experience, the interaction of the players and what's really going on. Very few people do that, especially these days."

Rick also said the Doors were the key artist of the L.A. sound of the '60s, and the Doors were his favorite band. And that the Doors and the Mamas and the Papas were guides that brought him into the Laurel Canyon neighborhood.

A: By the third album, *Waiting for the Sun*, Paul Rothchild was becoming a real Laurel Canyon connoisseur of veteran potent stuff that was being crossbred by the Northern California growers. All those guys up in Humboldt County. For recording sessions, Rothchild had two types of marijuana: Work dope and also playback dope, which was a little stronger for listening later. One of the benefits of being a known rock 'n' roll band.

Q: "Celebration of the Lizard" from *Waiting for the Sun* still resonates Morrison's lyrics are prophetic.

A: We were working in the future space. The Doors on their third album were in the future. And many things have come to pass that Jim Morrison wrote about.

Q: We are then led into *The Soft Parade*, recorded at Elektra Studios. Was there a pre-production meeting where everyone voted to include the use of strings and horns on the album?

A: We had made three albums with the same formation, and at some point or another when you make albums you want to do an album with expanded sound. So you want to have some horns and strings. My God, everybody did it. And we were gonna do it too. I want some strings. I want some jazz arrangements. I want some classical arrangements. And everyone said yes. Great idea. And a record label that said it was fine. What was great about the record label was that Jac Holzman said, "Boys, do whatever you want. Just don't use the seven illegal words." George Carlin's seven forbidden words. Other than that, anything goes. Whatever you want to do. And Paul Rothchild encouraged it.

Q: And you're at the new Elektra Studios as well.

A: We have left Sunset Sound. The first two there and the third at T.T.G. on Sunset and Highland in Hollywood. We then went into Elektra's new place. Fabulous. It was all wooden. Brand-new state-of-the-art facility. We thought it was great and would be able to play there for free. I mean, after all, it was really the studio that the Doors built. "Jac, this is gonna be great," when he showed it to us. "And we get to record here for free." Jac said, "Free? No. You don't get to record here for free. But, I'll tell you what I'll do. For you guys, a 10 percent discount." [Laughs.] But it was a great recording studio and they had a great funky organ in there. Gnarly organ.

Q: As a teenager, I saw the Doors eating at Norm's Restaurant on La Cienega Boulevard. Located on the same street as Elektra Records. I was too young to even know you guys were recording. I didn't say hello. My mother remarked, "Let them eat. They're on the clock." I didn't quite know then what she meant. At the time she was typing scripts for *The Monkees* television series at Raybert Productions at the Columbia Pictures Gower Gulch movie studio.

A: Absolutely. It was work. We didn't fool around. We were working. We're recording. The clock is ticking. This is your job. Your job starts at 2:00 p.m. in the afternoon and goes to 11:00 at night, 12 or one o'clock in the morning. You go home. You go to bed. You get up the next day. Maybe at 11:00 a.m. have a leisurely breakfast, take care of a couple of things and go back to the recording studio. Because guess what, Harvey, the recording studio is the only place you wanted to be. I didn't want to see anybody. I didn't want to go to a film or a jazz club. I wanted to make records. Right then and right there. With Jim Morrison, Robby Krieger, John Densmore, Paul Rothchild, Bruce Botnick and Doug Lubahn. Great bass player.

Q: George Harrison dropped by one of your *Soft Parade* sessions. He was visiting the Elektra studios. He mentioned all the musicians reminded him of the Beatles' *Sgt. Pepper's* because of the orchestra booked and percussion instruments.

A: Yes. A Beatle in the room. A very charming guy. Very low-key. And I'm surprised John Densmore didn't become good friends with him.

Q: And, once again, the Morrison vocals are potent, distinctive, and his voice more confident than ever.

A: He's no longer a blues singer. He's added Frank Sinatra crooning to his voice and did an absolutely brilliant job. Terrific. Girls loved it. "Touch Me," a No. 1 song.

Q: You also had individual writing credits for the first time on the album sleeve.

Robby Krieger and Ray Manzarek December 1969
Photo by Henry Diltz

A: That's a great story. Because of "Touch Me." The song was initially called "Hit Me," and Jim is gonna say "hit me." It's "Hit Me" like in poker. And Jim said, "No, it's not like poker. It's like someone is gonna walk up to me and are gonna hit me. You gotta change the line." "To what?" "Touch Me." Beautiful. Morrison, a military boy, said, "I am not going to say that." And Robby replied, "That's the way I wrote it, and you can't change it." Robby was going to stand up to Jim at that point. And Jim did. And Robby said, "Well, that's the song." And Jim said, "We're gonna have to say that you wrote this song." And Robby said, "OK. Fine with me." And that lasted for one or two more albums.

Q: And, guitarist Robby Krieger was another kind of songwriter. He penned a lot of the popular radio hits and chart singles. "Love Me Two Times," "Spanish Caravan," the lyrics

34

to "Tell All the People," "Touch Me," "Runnin' Blue," "Love Her Madly," and co-wrote "Peace Frog" and "Light My Fire" with Morrison.

A: Robby was a different sort of lyric writer. You know, Robby might be the secret weapon of the Doors, we get this great guitar player who plays bottleneck, and all of a sudden he comes in and plays "Light My Fire," the first song he ever co-wrote with Jim. Another guy with a high IQ.

Q: On *The Soft Parade* you had Harvey Brooks as well as Doug Lubahn on bass, saxophonist Curtis Amy, and George Bohannon the trombonist.

A: Curtis Amy, who was married to Merry Clayton. Curtis was a big nationally known jazz horn player who lived in Los Angeles. He takes the solo on "Touch Me." It might have been the first time a real jazz saxophone solo went to No. 1 on pop charts. And, we brought the strings and horn players to some shows and TV appearances. It was a great deal of fun for me to bring them on stage.

It didn't work for a lot of the critics and teenagers. "We're not coming to see you guys expand. We want to see 'Light My Fire.' Four Doors. The sexy lead singer. You play the songs. No horns. No strings. No jazz soloing." Well, you're gonna get it anyway.

Q: And by *The Soft Parade* Jim Morrison started to really indulge in drink.

A: Jimbo came out. They call it the demon rum. There's a demon in the bottle.

And there's a demon in that white powder, too. A demon on the blade. You know what those things do? They open the trap door of the subconscious and allow some creature to come out. And the alcohol for Jim, a genetic predisposition, family predisposition to alcohol, something came out, man. Some kind of combination. He went from being the poet to a shooter. Shooter Morrison. I was flabbergasted.

We started experimenting in the studio. I wouldn't allow anything to get out of the recording studio without my approval. If I didn't think it was right, it did not go on a record. Nothing happened without my OK. We did some composite vocals. You do what you have to do. If Jim sings one line, great. Fine. Then let's get the next line. Let's get the words, man. Whatever it takes to get the best possible performance.

While you can see that Jim Morrison is undergoing a transformation. Right before our very eyes. And I hoped that this transformation was short-lived. But it wasn't. "This can't last. This is not Jim."

The "Soft Parade" song is an unusual piece of music. It's a suite, you know. A suite of tunes all put together. Which is what it was.

Q: The Doors then arrive at *Morrison Hotel*. Why this direction?

A: Well, we had done our horns and strings experimentation. We had had a great time. I had a great time. Critically it was our least acclaimed album. However, it has stood the test of time, and there are many great songs on there. So, you know what? We've done that experimentation. Let's go back to the blues. Let's get dark and funky. Let's go downtown for the album cover.

We went to the Hard Rock Café on skid row with photographer Henry Diltz. And we went to a flophouse called the Morrison Hotel. Rooms, a sign read, $2.50 and up.

It was definitely supposed to be a funky album, and you can see that on the inside photo and the front and back cover. Album covers were always important. We were involved heavily in that process. You could never just turn it over to the record company. Everything that the Doors turned out had to be stamped by the Doors. We approve of this.

Q: There's a song called "Waiting for the Sun" on *Morrison Hotel.*

A: We loved the title. But the song had not come together earlier. We finally got it and a beautiful piece of music. It needed to cook more. Sometimes Doors songs came out of the collective conscious whole. "Bam. That's it." Others needed to cook and they needed be worked on. And "Waiting for the Sun" was one of those songs with a great title and the song took a while to jell.

Q: Morrison's voice lends itself to this specific material.

A: It was a barrelhouse album and barrelhouse singing. He's smoking cigarettes. "Jesus Christ, Jim. Do you have to smoke cigarettes and drink booze?" He didn't say it, but it was like, "This is what a blues man does." "Oh, fuck. That's right. You're an old blues man." And Rick and the Ravens was a surf and blues band from the South Bay. 'Roadhouse Blues.'
    That's Jim Morrison. Not Jimbo. Jimbo was the guy who took Jim to Paris and said, "Let's go and die in Paris." We're going to have a death in Paris. Like Thomas Mann's novella *Death in Paris.* That was Jimbo.
    "Peace Frog" is obviously about the 1968 Democratic Convention in Chicago. It was written after the young people rioted against the war in Vietnam. So it's the idea that blood is the cleansing property, and from blood will come the healing and the enlightenment of the nation. America is what Jim is singing about. And the mention of *Birth of a Nation.* Another cinematic reference.

37

The album was definitely blues, Raymond Chandler, downtown Los Angeles, Dalton Trumbo, John Fante, *City of Night,* John Rechy.

Q: In 1970 *The Doors Absolutely Live* came out...

A: We had a small tour of about seven or eight cities and decided to record five: New York, Boston, Philadelphia, Pittsburgh and Detroit. The original reason for the recording was so that the people could hear the Doors improvise, get the sense of stepping into the psychic unknown.

There were improvisations in the recording studio but within their soloing sections. And quite frankly, I never knew what I was going to play. I knew the chord changes. I didn't know how I was going to structure my A minor 7th chord. That would vary from take to take. It would always be an A minor 7th and in the groove. So there was improvisation in the studio, but here was major improvisation live. Because that's the whole point of live. You have the record as your foundation, and then you build upon that in the live performance.

Q: Just before the album *L.A. Woman* formally began, producer Paul Rothchild leaves the project.

A: Yes. He did a great service to us. We played the songs in the studio so Paul could hear what the songs were. First at the rehearsal studio, and then over to Elektra. I think we went back to Sunset Sound, too. We were bored. He was bored. We played badly. And Paul said, "You know what, guys? There's nothing here I can do. I'm done. You're gonna have to do it yourselves." And he walked out the door.

We looked at each other and said, "Shit. Bummer." And Bruce [Botnick] said, "Hey, I'll do it! I'll be the producer." John [Densmore] said, "We'll co-produce with you." Bruce said, "That's a deal. Let's all do it together." And then Jim said, "Can we record at our rehearsal studio?" And we all said, "Hey, we play great at our rehearsal studio. Let's do it. Can it be done?" And Bruce said, "Of course I can do it there. I'll set the board up and a studio upstairs. You guys record downstairs. That's where we'll make the album, and it will be virtually live." "Yeah!" And we got excited like that Mickey Rooney and Judy Garland "Let's put on a show!"

Q: Jerry Scheff plays bass on *L.A. Woman.*

A: Botnick brings in a guy who is going to be playing with Elvis Presley. "I got Elvis Presley's bass player." "Shit, man." He came in. A very cool guy who is playing with Elvis Presley.

Q: *L.A. Woman* is a logical step from *Morrison Hotel.*

A: I think it's the same Doors but a continual growth, continual evolution of the Doors. Continual revolution of the Doors.

Q: The title track, "L.A. Woman," embodies movement, freedom, lust and dust.

A: "L.A. Woman" is just a fast L.A. kickass freeway driving song in the key of A with barely any chord changes at all. And it just goes. It's like Neal Cassady, Jack Kerouac and Allen Ginsberg heading from L.A. up to Bakersfield on the 5 freeway. Let's go, man.
        I saw Al Kooper's new band at the time, Blood, Sweat & Tears, at The Café Au Go-Go in Greenwich Village, New York, and it was probably the best use of horns we'd ever seen up to that point in rock 'n' roll or since then. He captured the essence of the four horns with guitar, bass, drums and keyboard absolutely superbly. I play, at the end of my piano

solo on "L.A. Woman," my homage and tip of the hat to Al Kooper. I play a musical quote from "House in the Country."

"Riders on the Storm." It's the final classic, man. Interestingly, Robby and Jim come in and were working on "Riders on the Storm." And then they start to play it and it sounded like "Ghost Riders in the Sky." No. We don't do anything like "Ghost Riders in the Sky," as much as I like it by Vaughn Monroe. And Jim likes it. What's next? A version of Frankie Laine's "Mule Train"? Doors don't do that. Let's make this hip. The idea is good. We're going to go out on the desert. This has got to be dark, strange and moody. Let me see what I can do here. It was like "Light My Fire." It just came to me. I got it. The bass line. It became this dark, moody Sunset Strip 1948 jazz joint. That highway and freeway chase.

The storm is an unresolved psyche. We are moving into the Jungian collective unconscious. And those motivations in the collective unconscious are the same in 1976, 1968, 1969 as they are in 1994, 1995. There are needs that we all have on the human planet, and we must satisfy those needs and come to grips with the darkness and the interior of the human psyche.

Q: And only Morrison could inject a Hollywood movie studio system reference lyrically about an actor being loaned to another film company.

A: Yeah. How 'bout that, man.

Q: In 2007 for *Goldmine* magazine we talked about Doors recordings utilized in movies, and the film school influence is obvious again, especially on "L'America" on *Morrison Hotel.*

A: It was written for the director Michelangelo Antonioni for his film *Zabriskie Point.* And we played it for him at the rehearsal studio and backed him up against the wall with the volume. We played it the way we normally play and too loud for this elderly Italian gentleman. I could see him pressed up against the door trying to get out of the place. We finish the song, he slides the door open and steps outside, and it was almost like he was saying, "Goodbye, boys. Goodbye, Hollywood." And then he goes with Pink Floyd. It was all too much for him. He just couldn't do it.

Q: Besides the supplemental exposure a movie and subsequent soundtrack collection brings to one of your recordings and the economic gain, what kind of feelings do you get when you hear and see one of your songs taken out of the original context it was written and recorded in?

A: Here's what it is from my perspective. This is my relationship to it. It always becomes the matter of the art. The art is the important thing. What is being communicated to the people who are listening to or watching and listening to the art form. You are taking the Doors songs, and the Doors always tried to make those songs as artistic as they possibly could. It was never a commercial attempt, it was an artistic attempt.

Now, if you take that artistic attempt and couple it, the synchronization, you can synchronize that with an artistic vision of images on the screen, that's the best of all possible worlds. When it works, like in *Apocalypse Now*, at the beginning, it works like a champ. And it's absolutely delightful. To sit back in an audience and hear "The End" come on in the beginning of *Apocalypse Now*, and see the jungle go up in napalm, it's absolutely thrilling from an artistic standpoint. Film school guys founded the Doors. When we made the music, each song had to have a dramatic structure.

Each song, whether it was two and a half minutes or an epic like "The End" or "When the Music's Over," you had to have dramatic peaks and valleys, and that's the sense of drama within the Doors' songs which comes right from the theater. The point of art is to blow minds.

Q: In 2006 you have a huge box set, *Perception.*

A: We thought we would re-EQ and remaster everything to celebrate our 40th anniversary and bring out a super-duper box set. We added a bunch of bonus material, some you haven't heard before, then Bruce Botnick, genius that he is, does a surround sound 5.1 mix of all the studio albums. Not only the studio albums as stereo, but surround sound mixes, complete with video along with the audio. I'm a fan of 5.1. But it's an art form that hasn't found itself yet. Quite frankly, for me it's a delivery system. I'm the guy who plays the introduction to "Light My Fire." I create the music, how it's delivered to the audience... One day it's gonna be delivered on a little chip, for God's sake. But that doesn't concern me as much as the art of the music.

And, with the box set you get 12 videos, so we like to marry the music and visual art forms. On the box there is a never-before-seen Doors in the studio during the *L.A. Woman* recording sessions: An Australian film crew was present and they were shooting the Doors, and now we have the Doors performing John Lee Hooker's 'Crawling King Snake.' Man, where does this stuff come from? I have no memory of them being there. I don't know where it came from.

Someone happened to mention 'Hey... Australian TV has a version of you guys doing "Crawling King Snake." "What?" "Send it over!"

Q: What is it like for you to hear the *Perception* collection?

A: Harvey, I was there when "My Eyes Have Seen You" was actually recorded. I walked out of the studio into the control room and heard it back on the magnificent speakers, brand-new, fresh recorded. So I'm spoiled under the best conditions possible. But what we've tried to do is to approximate for you, the listener, for the audience, those conditions. We try and make it sound as close to that original thing as it can possibly get.

And I gotta tell you, man, the whole box set sounds as close as being in the recording studio with the Doors as you're ever going to be. It's state-of-the-art fidelity. Bruce Botnick just makes it more and more alive as the technology gets better and better. As alive as you're really gonna hear it. Really revolutionary. When you hear the surround sound, you are in the recording studio with the Doors. If you have half a brain and you can get past the Lizard King and just listen to the art of Jim Morrison.

That's all we want you to do. He would not want you to be enamored and swept up in this worship of Jim Morrison, this monster in black leather pants, the snake man, the Lizard King. Listen: "I'm a poet, would you just listen to me sing my words?" When I first heard Jim sing in Venice I thought he had it. There was no doubt that he would not have any problems 'cause the microphone is no problem. Pitch is the problem with a singer.

Can you sing in the same key on pitch? And I worked with a lot of singers who can't do that. Finding the notes. But Morrison had a good sense of pitch. So, if it was in the key of G, he would sing "Moonlight Drive" in the key of G. And he would be there right on pitch. That was the important thing. The rest of it was all acquired expertise in your practice of your instrument.

So, what happens with the playing of Doors music, you enter at a lower state of consciousness into an almost hypnotic state and at the same time an elevated cosmic state of consciousness. So you are cosmically aware and you are hypnotically down into the vibrations, the energy of the telluric force, the energy of the planet, the energy of the

43

thousand-miles-an-hour spinning globe that we're on. With that hot molten center. You're part of that and you're part of the infinite cosmos at the same time. All in playing music. And that's what Doors music is about. It's right there.

Q: Let's discuss the 2006 retrospective coffee table book *The Doors by the Doors* with Ben Fong-Torres, published by Hyperion. It's a joint effort, and it's the first time the remaining members of the band have collaborated to offer commentary on your legacy. I interviewed Ben, who told me everyone was cooperative and candid and that "The big surprises were from Jim's family. Admiral George Morrison, who'd been depicted as being so opposed to his son's rock career, spoke of his pride in what Jim had achieved. You only wish that Jim had been able to hear it for himself."

A: Well, Ben Fong-Torres is an old buddy from way back from when he was an editor at *Rolling Stone*. For this book he interviewed everybody, previously Jim Morrison, and now the Admiral Morrison, who speaks for the very first time. What Ben has done is present everyone in their own perspective on how it all took place. We talk about the Doors, and in a way, you as the reader come to your own conclusions. What is the true story? I find that fascinating. What's great about having another guy there like Ben involved is that he brings his perspective to the whole thing and ties it up from an outsider's point of view. I'm locked into the stories I tell, the stories I know, and the way I want the Doors to be viewed. But Ben views it as an outsider; that makes it a whole unique book with an outside perspective. I live up in Northern California [Napa Valley] and Ben is in San Francisco, so he would come over to my house with a tape recorder. And we'd work face to face, and he did this with everybody. I'm telling you, there are some photos—"Where did this come from? Where did this come from?" Things I'd never seen before. The photos are incredible and fabulous.

Q: There's also a new companion book, *The Doors: The Complete Illustrated Lyrics*, edited by Danny Sugerman, who worked for and with the Doors for decades, and who chronicled the band, along with Jerry Hopkins, in the book *No One Here Gets Out Alive.*

A: Danny Sugerman, late of planet Earth, now at the roadhouse in the sky with all the rest of the rockers up there, put that book together, and this is a reissue and a reformatted version of that book. Danny Sugerman was the office boy who worked his way all the way up to becoming the manager of the Doors. And a good Sammy Glick. He was ambitious but not insane like Sammy Glick. Danny was great fun to work with plotting strategies on how to make the world remember the Doors. This is after Morrison's death. "Man, here's our job, Danny. Jim is dead, the Doors have closed up. I left the Doors. We are going to make the world remember the Doors and Jim Morrison. Now, they may not like Jim Morrison, but they will remember the name of Jim Morrison." "Let's do it."

Q: What do you sign and autograph besides your memoir *Light My Fire: My Life with the Doors* at personal appearances?

A: Well, everybody loves the first album, *The Doors*, and *L.A. Woman.* Those are our best-selling albums. But invariably, I'm signing *Strange Days.* A lot of people come with their CDs, but a lot of the old-timers come with their albums.

So, I'm invariably signing the inside of *L.A. Woman,* and the inside of *Morrison Hotel,* where we're sitting in the bar. They love *Morrison Hotel* and *Strange Days.* I think those are the two albums I sign the most.

Q: Let's talk about *The Doors* movie, directed by Oliver Stone, who took some liberties, including facts about Jim Morrison's life at the UCLA film school. As you of all people know, Morrison did not drop out or quit UCLA, as depicted in Stone's biopic. He graduated. Jim's parents wouldn't have paid the rent on his Goshen Avenue Westwood apartment without that college degree!

A: Exactly! [Laughs.] Val Kilmer did a wonderful job. Ray Manzarek goes on record as saying Val Kilmer did a wonderful job as Jim Morrison. The rock 'n' roll scenes were real good, and maybe the first half-hour of the movie was very good. But the rest of it just sucked. The problem with the movie is that Oliver Stone doesn't know what psychedelics are.

Q: Was it awkward watching yourself portrayed onscreen?

A: Well, yes. The fellow who played me, I felt was rather stiff and wooden. [Laughs.] And I would highly recommend a serious session with some hemp. I think some hemp would have loosened him up very, very nicely and he would have been a lot more spontaneous.

Q: This century you've seen changes in marijuana legislation and law enforcement.

A: I didn't grow up with reefer madness and paranoia. I was a musician. I initially knew it from guys who were jazz musicians and smoked it. Then, all of a sudden, it makes its appearance in the world of the '60s, you know. "Holy cow!" It's like everyone is smoking a joint now. It's like no big deal at all. A common occurrence. It's God's good green earth that grows on God's good clean planet. And it's a mild intoxicant.

46

A slight hallucinogenic. It's not LSD or peyote or mushrooms. It's got a little bit of consciousness expansion. And I think it's virtually harmless. And it makes for a much more tranquil, benign society. Without people being at each other's throats as they are with alcohol. Marijuana is just a relaxant that enhances reality. Now what on earth is wrong with that? Why is it illegal? I have no idea why it is illegal. To this day I still don't know. I'm all in favor of decriminalization.

I mean, I'd legalize it. But I think you can't go that far all at once. You just decriminalize it. And the pot clubs, I think, are terrific. A great idea. Medical marijuana is a great idea. I'm all for it.

The Doors London Fog, 1967
CaveHollywood.com, 2016

In 1967, the Doors were the house band at the London Fog, a Sunset Strip dive bar located just footsteps away from the Whisky a Go Go, the future home of the group's most chronicled performances.

The Doors open a virtual time capsule with *London Fog 1966*, a Collector's Edition box set that features unearthed audio recorded at the club in May 1966. Previously unreleased and not even known to exist until recently, this marks the earliest recordings of the band and finds the quartet mixing blues covers with early versions of Doors originals.

London Fog 1966 is an individually numbered limited edition of 18,000 copies. Additionally, there's a postcard, the set list handwritten by John Densmore, and a program for the Royce Hall UCLA student film screening.

Presented in a lift-top package designed to look like a vintage storage box, the set features seven songs on both CD and a 10-inch record that's made to resemble a test pressing. Noted Doors engineer Bruce Botnick recently mastered the audio for this collection.

Nettie Peña, one of the lucky few to be in attendance at the London Fog for this fabled show, was a pivotal force in this release coming together, as she captured the audio on a ¼" reel-to-reel recorder, which was the property of the Los Angeles Unified School District. Her father was a teacher for LAUSD and let her borrow the recorder to take to the show.

During their residency at the London Fog, the Doors frequently worked out new songs onstage that would eventually appear on various studio albums. At this show, the band played two originals. The first, "Strange Days," would become the title track for the band's second studio album, which came out in 1967. This is one of the only known live recordings of this track. The other Doors original, "You Make Me Real," wasn't officially released on a studio album until *Morrison Hotel* in 1970.

"To hear 'Strange Days,' that came out on their second album, in almost final shape so early on was truly amazing," says Jac Holzman, the president of Elektra Records who signed the Doors to their multi-album recording contract.

Kim Fowley, 2007

Early in 1965 I recorded a song, "The Trip" in one take in the middle of El Monte with a group of pickup musicians. There was a Farfisa organ on the record. My original version was released on Corby Records, which is a defunct label out of Oregon who put it out. It was later covered by Godfrey on the C Jam label. I put one of the 500 copies that were manufactured into the hands of Jesse, the manager/owner/bartender of the London Fog, who thought it was a good song and put it into the jukebox.

When the Doors showed up a year later, they used it as their "break song." Jesse would play it and it would be the signal for them to take their break from the bandstand. And if you hear a song for multiple weeks or months, it will get into your subconscious and it will influence you.

Albert Goldman many years ago came to interview me when he was researching a book on Jim Morrison. Once of the things he mentioned to me, knowing I casually knew some of the band members, having been onstage with them a couple of times, was that he obtained the BMI or ASCAP logged reports on "The Trip" and the frequent airplays it received in 1965–1967 on the jukebox at the London Fog. He was a good researcher. Some people have cited that "The Trip" might have had some influence on the Doors' "Soul Kitchen."

I first saw the Doors when they were an opening act and unsigned band at Ciro's on Sunset. There was a heckler in the audience who ridiculed the three musician Doors as they loaded their own instruments on stage and amps, and wanted to pick a fight with them. And he was doing a theatrical heckler improv, and then jumped up to show them that he as an audience member could be a better singer than their missing singer, who was probably hiding in the dressing room or outside in the street out of fear. And then Jim Morrison did "Break On Through." That was the first song. The place went wild. Because no one had ever seen them before.

I saw the Doors everywhere. I introduced them at the Devonshire Downs Meadows Raceway in Northridge at Valley State College in July 1967. It was the Fantasy Faire & Magic Music Festival. Astounding. They had magic.

Jim could sing in pitch, he had the image and the poetry. He understood theater. Ray's organ was a music box to a volcano. Manzarek supplied a pulse, and Robby the guitarist is never given credit what he brought to the table in 1967. John Densmore was a jazz drummer. You also had a jazz keyboardist and a jazz guitarist all playing the blues with a real great poet and actor fronting it. It was tremendous. It was theater.

49

Dave Diamond, 2009

Jim Morrison was the best white-person performer. Better than Elvis. Better than Jagger. Because he did what Howlin' Wolf and Lawrence Olivier did. Morrison did it all at the same time. He did William Shakespeare and gutbucket together. And only P.J. Proby rivaled him, and David Bowie came in third.

The Doors were not a rock 'n' roll band but gave you a rock 'n' roll feeling. And the only band that did that was the original King Crimson. 'Cause they weren't a rock 'n' roll band, either. But when you heard *Court of the Crimson King*, and Pink Floyd '67, they were the only bands who had some Wagner with a rock 'n' roll attitude.

Dave Diamond, 2009

I saw the Doors at the London Fog and the Whisky a Go Go. I played *The Doors* LP acetate on my KBLA *Diamond Mine* show. The Doors did a couple of high school gigs for me. I spun selections from their album along with numerous tracks from Love. In early 1966 I had telephoned Jac Holzman and mentioned the Doors to him.

"Break On Through," their first single, really didn't make it. Robby [Krieger] and John [Densmore] come over to my Los Feliz place, checking my fan mail and reading all the letters [that said,] "Play the Doors!" I'd get 50 or 60 letters a day, 'cause I was spinning this new stuff. People were just going nuts. They never had heard this kind of music.

One day, they come over, and they are both all sullen and gloom. "'Break On Through' stiffed. We don't know what to do, and the record company won't do this and that." I said, "Have them put out 'Light My Fire.'" They replied, "They won't do it because it's too long. No one will play that long a record."

So I took them over to KBLA and showed them how to edit it down, removing the long instrumental passage. "Take

50

that to Jac Holzman, and you'll have a No. 1 hit." And that's what they did.

Jac Holzman, 2017

As for the debut Doors album, [producer] Paul Rothchild and I discussed how far we should take 'em. He said, "Well, why don't we take them to 80 percent of concert pitch and let them come in the studio." "That sounds great to me." So that's what we did.

Jim and Arthur Lee were interesting characters. Jim Morrison died young. Jimmy Dean. That's part of it. But Jim lived his life as full and he lived his life without any attention to convention, or what anybody else thought, and a flame that bright usually does not burn long.

Arthur admired the Doors. And he was the one who said, "You ought to stay around for their Whisky a Go Go show. That band is pretty good."

Now I stay around for the Doors' show in March of 1966. When I saw them, I heard a lot of blues, and I didn't need any more white blues singers. And the band did not feel that comfortable. The Doors could do the blues, but it was later when I heard the adventurousness of their approach of taking something like "The Alabama Song" and converting it so it could be done as a rock-infused song. That told me a lot.

I was more impressed by Ray Manzarek at the beginning than I was by Jim. Jim had the vocal chops, but that persona crept out once he knew he had a safe home or a safe perch to work from.

Remember: The Doors were a band that had been signed to Columbia [Records] and they couldn't even get to make a single. And the reason I offered them a three-album guarantee was that I never wanted them to feel that they would get booted out the door if the first LP didn't sell. So that was the genesis of that. "What can I do that nobody else is crazy enough to do?"

There were two Doors albums out in 1967. Which was unusual, but it was done on purpose to get them really established as an act and not as a one-album wonder. So we had the first album that came out in January, and then we had *Strange Days*, which came out in October, and recorded in summer."

My part of the creative process is to be involved but not buried in the middle to the extent that I lost my perception or position to be able to look at it from slightly afar. So as to determine what we got was what I thought was going to work. And album covers were important to the sale of music.

I saw myself as a midwife to their music. They recorded it. I helped supervise how it was going to be taken in and what I hoped would be willing ears. That's my job. And it's my job to talk tough when I need to. But I never had that kind of problem with the Doors.

The only time was when there was much screaming about Miami. I said, "If your shows are being canceled, we will figure something out about how we're going to bring you back live. In the meantime, go into the studio and start writing another album." And that was *Morrison Hotel*.

And then we did two evenings of Doors concerts at the Aquarius Theater on Sunset Boulevard and those tickets were two dollars. We underwrote the rest. We picked up the tab. But it was there where we launched them. And that idea came from us. That's kind of what you do when you live your artists' anguish and you try and help them and you over the tough spots.

The Doors *Live at the Matrix, 1967*

Rhino and Bright Midnight Archives in 2008 present *Live at the Matrix 1967*, the latest installment in the Doors' series of archival concert releases. This two-disc addition to the band's live canon contains two club shows witnessed by few but bootlegged by many.

Restored and carefully mastered from first-generation tapes acquired by Elektra Records and the Doors 40 years ago, these historic shows never sounded better. The package features cover art by Stanley Mouse.

Live at the Matrix 1967 rewinds to the band's early days for a pair of shows at a San Francisco club that March.

Only a handful of people showed up, so Jim Morrison, John Densmore, Robby Krieger, and Ray Manzarek played for each other, exploring song arrangements and jamming on a few blues favorites.

"San Francisco was quiet where we kinda scared everybody," John Densmore mentioned in a 2007 interview we did for a *MOJO '60s* issue. "I could tell they liked us—we were the underbelly. You forget, in the Summer of Love, there is the Vietnam War on everyone's mind. They stared at us like we were from Mars. We knew that was making an impact."

In spite of the empty room, the band is fully engaged, using the time to give "The End" and "Back Door Man" extra lyrics and extended sections. "This is probably the closest we've come to a true document of the Doors without constraints," says Bruce Botnick, the album's producer and the band's longtime co-producer and engineer.

The band performs much of its self-titled debut on the first disc, including "Soul Kitchen," "Alabama Song (Whisky Bar)," and the first single, "Break On Through (To the Other Side)." Along with those early originals, the band indulges its love of the blues with Bo Diddley's "Who Do You Love," Muddy Waters's "I'm a King Bee," and Allen Toussaint's "Get Out of My Life, Woman," which has never appeared on any previous Doors albums.

The second disc offers a glimpse of the band mapping out its future, working out early versions of several songs from upcoming albums: "Crawling King Snake" (*L.A. Woman*); "Summer's Almost Gone" (*Waiting for the Sun*); and nearly half of the songs from the Doors' second album, *Strange Days*.

Dennis Loren, 2017

Two friends and I arrived in San Francisco, California, on the 4th of March, 1967, after a four-day road trip from Detroit, Michigan, in my 1965 Falcon. We had taken turns driving and made pretty good time crossing the country, stopping only for gas, meals and one flat tire—ha!!! One of us would sleep in the back seat, while one drove and the other rode shotgun. Once we reached San Francisco, the three of us went our separate ways. Each of us had our own destinations and places to stay. The next day—after getting a good night's sleep—I began exploring the City. One of my main goals was tracking down all of the great music venues that I had heard about. One of the first places I found was the Matrix.

Over the next few years, the Matrix would become one of my favorite venues. Marty Balin and three partners had opened the club in 1965 to showcase Marty's band Jefferson Airplane. The Matrix was located in the Cow Hollow district of San Francisco—not far from Lombard Street and the Marina district—at 3138 Fillmore Street.

In those days, posters, handbills, flyers and word of mouth were how a person found out about the different concerts around town. You would have to get to the venue early and stand in line to get a ticket. There were no ticket agencies or internet.

The very first concert I saw at the Matrix featured the Doors. This was kind of ironic, because in February, just before I left, a Detroit friend had played me the group's debut album, which I found had a unique and extremely intriguing sound. The Doors were booked for a five-day stand at the Matrix, beginning on March 7 and ending on March 11, 1967. I attended the show on Thursday evening, March 9. There was already a fairly long line outside the club, but I managed to get inside. I shared a table with three other people I had met in the line. Everyone seemed to be excited about seeing and hearing the Doors. The place was buzzing with anticipation as the group hit the stage.

The sound of the Doors was immediately mesmerizing. They began with the song "Break On Through (To the Other Side)," followed by "Soul Kitchen." In the course of the two sets I was there for, they played an interesting mix of original songs from the first album ("Alabama Song," "The End" and others) and a few cover songs that included "Money," "Who Do You Love," "I'm a King Bee," "Gloria" and, most surprisingly, "Summertime." Of course my favorite songs were "Crystal Ship" and "Light My Fire."

Watching and listening to the magical interplay of keyboard player Ray Manzarek, guitarist Robby Krieger, drummer John Densmore and singer Jim Morrison was nothing short of amazing. Especially considering that I was only about 15 feet from the stage. The ambience of the room and sound was—in my opinion—always great. You had to be there—ha!!! As I recall the Doors also played the song "People Are Strange," before its release on their second album.

While the group was in San Francisco that March, the Doors would also perform at the Family Dog's Avalon Ballroom. During this stage of their career the group seemed to frequent venues and festival events in the San Francisco Bay Area numerous times. On what now seems like an almost monthly basis, I would get to see the Doors several more times during 1967, including their set at the Magic Mountain Music Festival across the Golden Gate Bridge on Mount Tamalpias in Marin County.

Dr. James Cushing, 2007

By July, the Doors' "Light My Fire" would be a big hit and join other songs, such as Jefferson Airplane's "Somebody to Love" and "White Rabbit," the Youngbloods' "Get Together," Procol Harum's "Whiter Shade of Pale" and Scott McKenzie's "San Francisco" as anthems for the Summer of Love.

As a postscript, I should mention that Peter Abrams would record the Doors' Matrix shows on March 7 and 10.

As an interesting aside, the central image of the winged statue that artist Stanley Mouse used on the CD cover had been previously been used by Mouse on one of five posters created for San Francisco light show pioneer Bill Ham's 40th-anniversary performance. The other four posters were designed by Alton Kelley, David Singer, the team of Chuck Sperry & Ron Donovan and myself.

Dr. James Cushing, 2007

The Doors radiated a sexual heat that evoked ancient blood rituals. Morrison's poetry formed one part of a larger theater-music-performance that climaxed when tragic heroism blossomed up out of his intimate Freudian night-garden.

The Doors' first two records almost captured that dark bloom, and they retain great power to disturb us with their shadowy images of private life palpably heightened to the realm of myth. When the band performed, they also had a jazz flexibility in their set lists. The 1967 Matrix club repertoire and their Hollywood Bowl summer '68 concert are examples of that.

The Doors at the Matrix in March 1967 were remarkable in many ways. Essential for anyone into the Doors, because their debut album had been out but not yet very well known. You can tell by the clapping that they might be playing to an audience as much as 25 people max. It has the feeling of a more than intimate rehearsal than a concert. Since it's more of an intimate, almost a living room concert, and the recording, B-plus, A-minus as it is, conveys some of it, the intimacy of the recording allows them to try things out that they wouldn't be able to try out later. And one of those great things is a nine-minute instrumental version of "Summertime" on the second disc.

And when I saw the title mentioned on the back of the album, "Boy. I get to hear Jim Morrison sing 'Summertime,' because that would be great because Janis Joplin sang it on *Cheap Thrills*." But this turns out to be an instrumental version of it featuring a terrific jazz solo by keyboardist Ray Manzarek. And a terrific Kenny Burrell informed by Robby Krieger, with John Densmore's drums keeping that good Donald Bailey vibe. It was written by the Gershwin brothers for *Porgy and Bess*. Miles Davis did it, Ella Fitzgerald did it. It's been a jazz standard for many years, and to see it appear by the Doors and Big Brother and the Holding Company is a remarkable gesture, you might say, from the new school back to the old. A kind of a valentine from the younger generation to the music of their parents' generation.

"Summertime" recalls and anticipates a lot of what they did on their debut album, but it also makes the claim of the Doors as stealth jazz band even more believable.

Paul Body, 2007

I saw the Doors at my former high school, Monrovia. The Merry-Go-Round opened. I didn't have a ticket since I wasn't a student. So after talking to their guitarist Robby Krieger, he had me carry his guitar into the auditorium. I think they only did three songs—"Break On Through," they did twice.

Mark Guerrero, 2016

I was 18 years old and already having my own bands in East L.A. for five years by 1967 when the Doors' first album was released. "Light My Fire," which was included on that LP, was one of the quintessential songs and records of the Summer of Love. The Beatles' *Sgt. Pepper's Lonely Hearts Club Band* was the ubiquitous album of that memorable time.

Aside from my visit to Haight-Ashbury in San Francisco, my other enduring memory of that summer was being a passenger in my bass player Rick Rosas's 1962 Chevy Impala driving west on the Sunset Strip, unwittingly on my first acid trip, with "Light My Fire" blasting out of the car speakers. I say "unwittingly" because in that age of experimentation with substances, I took a pill a friend gave me he said was THC.

Knowing that compound was the main active ingredient of cannabis, I took it expecting to have no more than a pleasant pot high. It wasn't until a couple of years later when I "wittingly" took LSD did I realize what I was tripping on that night back in 1967. As Rick and I glided in his low-rider car by the Whisky a Go Go in what now felt like a spaceship, the neon lights on the Strip were unusually vibrant and colorful, while my consciousness was in a place it had never been. Somehow the perfect song for that moment and experience happened to come on the radio providing the soundtrack.

Rick Williams, 2017

My first Doors show was at the Hullabaloo, an after-hours show; the show began at 2:00 a.m., and the Doors played last, and were mind-blowingly amazing. The sun was rising as the show ended. I'd never seen anything remotely like what

David Dalton, 2018

they did that night. This was in the latter part of 1966, or maybe very early '67, no album out yet.

Most clubs, probably the London Fog among them, were age-21-and-over rooms, but not long after this, as I recall, the Whisky adjusted to an 18-and-over policy.

I'd seen the Doors four or five times. Among my own memories of the Crescenta Valley High show: definitely an afternoon show, though a 3:00 p.m. start time still sounds at least a little unrealistic (maybe 4 instead?) since school didn't get out until 3:15. Although, if it was part of the one day a school year event they called "The Day" (pronounced as "Thee," for reasons I never learned), maybe it was as early as three o'clock.

They opened the show, as they had the first time I ever saw them, with "When the Music's Over." I can very clearly recall Jim wrapping his leg around the mic stand, in what was an almost sexual stance (something I'd seen him do quite a few times by the date of this show). I also have a crystal-clear memory of the first thing out of his mouth being a fairly bloodcurdling, pretty primal-sounding scream, that caused one of the slightly older women instructors monitoring the show to be visibly shaken in shock/surprise.

The show began really strongly, and I was still just stunned that they were actually there, playing the high school. When technical problems cut things short, I was just all the more glad that I'd already gone to the effort to see them playing a number of times in Hollywood. At the time, there was no other band, even Love, that was as capable of absolutely mesmerizing an audience as the Doors.

David Dalton, 2018

I had gotten married to my bride, and we were on acid, and we had the party at Steve Paul's The Scene. And Morrison and the Doors were playing there that night. It had a tiny dressing room. I saw Morrison and said, "How are you doing?" And he said to me, "The universe is communicating with itself," and I assumed he was on acid. And, of course, I was on acid. And I responded, "Jim, I think we're on the same planet." [Laughs.]

The thing about Jim Morrison, the only times I ran into him, he was either raving or he was in his graduate student mode. And that was that night. There were his notebooks and he was scribbling. I kind of think of him as hunched over and very serious, earnest and, you know, the haunted poet.

Chris Darrow, 2016

After the English Invasion, I started a group called the Floggs, an all-electric band in the Yardbirds, Them, Animals, Stones mold. I was the writer and lead singer and became the bass player by default. We were guitar, bass, organ and drums. We did gigs with groups like the Rising Sons, with Ry Cooder and Taj Mahal, who were friends from the Ash Grove scene. We were very good and recorded a seven-song demo to shop.

My wife and I went to see the first U.S. gig by Them on a Thursday night at the Whiskey a Go Go. They were great, but there was an opening act that I just hated. A guy wearing leather and posturing who seemed to sing out of tune led them. The keyboard player was good and looked a little like John Sebastian. I went up to the owner, Elmer Valentine, and said, "I got a band better than this! Can I give you a tape?" We never got the gig; the band was the Doors.

In the winter of 1967 I was playing with Kaleidoscope in New York City and staying at a friend's pad on 111th and Broadway in Spanish Harlem. His name is Charlie Zetterberg, and he was going to Columbia Law School at the time. He is a great banjo player, and we were in a bluegrass band when I first met my Kaleidoscope bandmate David Lindley.

We had known each other in L.A. and we hung out a bit at our producer Barry Friedman's house on Fountain Avenue, where Jim was hustling Nico at the time. She, incidentally, was co-billed with Kaleidoscope at Steve Paul's The Scene.

I was just leaving the Kaleidoscope and was being courted by Jeff Hanna and John McEuen of the Nitty Gritty Dirt Band about joining their band. I saw them play in November 1967 at Hunter College co-billed with the Doors. Later as a group member I encountered Morrison and the Doors a number of times.

We did gigs together, but the most memorable of the meetings was in New York City. While backstage, I saw Jim, and he called me into his dressing room. He had a rather detached look on his face and flatly asked me, "Have you ever tried ether?" I said, "No man, never did," and he just stared at me until I walked out of the room.

John Densmore Interview
MOJO '60s magazine, 2007

Q: All through your entire Doors career, where did you learn to be both a support and lead musician?

A: I saw [drummer] Roy Haynes earlier this year. He's 80, and he's fuckin' stronger than me at my peak. And, I said, "Roy. I know your secret. And I'm into it too. Dynamics." It pulls people in. It's human. Very loud and very soft, rather than one level. I didn't know that. I just heard it.

When I wrote my autobiography [*Riders on the Storm: My Life with Jim Morrison and the Doors*], I took it to Elvin [Jones]. My hands were shaking. I mean, he's a jazz guy and I'm a rocker. I gave it to him, and inscribed, "Elvin, you gave me my hands." He was so sweet and flattered. By the end of his life I'm carrying his cymbals to the car at the Jazz Bakery. That's called mentorship.

John Densmore, December 20, 1969
Photo by Henry Diltz

Hearing jazz I first started with Dave Brubeck, then I saw Les McCann, blues and funk, Miles [Davis] and John Coltrane. At Valley State College one of the ethnological music instructors was Fred Katz, who was the cello player for the Chico Hamilton jazz quintet.

I saw Chico Hamilton at the Lighthouse. There was this ride cymbal riff that Chico did on a song. I stole one of his ride cymbal things that I used in "The End." Once I get to the kit and I'm playing the tambourine, it's Chico Hamilton. That's where it came from. Chico was direct. "Oh, that kind of cool cymbal riff, I think, would fit in that song," I was thinking to myself. Like, going into the bridge on "Wild Child," that's the press roll from Art Blakey. That was direct.

I was a jazz snob until I heard the moptops' music and I went, "They're cute." And then I got into rock 'n' roll. I saw every jazz great who ever came to town the first half of the 1960s. Les McCann at the Renaissance Club. Cannonball Adderley at Howard Rumsey's Lighthouse. Bill Evans five or six times at Shelly's Manne-Hole. I shook his hand. Harvey, Leroy Vinnegar played on "Spanish Caravan."

It's like when I saw Hendrix in 1967 at the Whisky just after the Monterey [International] Pop festival. God! We knew somebody was coming. A giant! It was just... I don't have the words... He was like Coltrane on guitar, playing it upside down, without changing the strings. Forget it.

I saw Coltrane many times. I noticed with Elvin Jones and John Coltrane there was communication. So, I thought, "I'm gonna keep the beat. That's our job as drummers. But I'm gonna try and talk to Jim during the music." Like, "When the Music's Over." That's Elvin. I knew I wasn't playing jazz.

Q: And, there is also the influence of film on your bandmates, and you were doing soundtrack coloring music in regards to your own playing.

A: I wasn't thinking cinematic, but certainly Ray and Jim, coming out of the UCLA film school, were cinematic dudes. That's for sure. I mean, I hear the world, filmmakers see it.

I went to Dick Bock's house in Laurel Canyon. I'm listening to Ravi Shankar records on his World Pacific label when I'm doing meditation. And then Dick Bock owes me a little time in the studio, so me, Jim and Ray make this little acetate at the World Pacific studio.

It's not lost on me when I walk in and there are tablas on the wall. I was scared. Dick Bock was incredibly generous, wore glasses. Dick was in TM before us with Clint Eastwood and Paul Horn. I'd run into Clint and say, "Hey man. You're a TM'er. I know you." "Yeah." There was still a little camaraderie in the early meditative circles. The very first TM class was with Clint Eastwood and Paul Horn the year before me. Paul later was in India with the Beatles.

Robby Krieger and I went to Ravi Shankar's School of Indian Music in between later Doors tours. I went to Professional Drum Shop and they had used cymbals. "What's this cracked piece of shit?" "Oh... That's Jimmy Cobb's old cymbal." "Oh! I'll take it." I like used old stuff that had personality.

I had to work harder on the tempo because Ray's left hand was the bass. And when he took a solo he'd get excited and speed up. "Hold it back. Hold it back." But, without a separate guy doing bass line runs and grooves there are holes. "OK. I'm going in." Sometimes I didn't do anything. That was my territory between the beats.

Let me tell you, at the Rock and Roll Hall of Fame [1993] induction, [Bruce] Springsteen came up to me and said, "I like your drumming. It's so quiet and then you drop a bomb." Thank you, Boss."

Q: Another thing about the Summer of Love, meditation started becoming more evident in popular culture and covered by the media, but in 1965, you and Robby met Ray Manzarek when you two went to the Transcendental Meditation Center in Los Angeles. You dudes were way early on this trip.

A: It's good for you to bring that in. TM was definitely Summer of Love. For some damn reason in 1965... Well, Robby and I went because LSD was legal and we were quite interested in our nervous systems, and knew we had to do this TM thing slowly. We go over there and I meet this little guy, Maharishi, and the "love vibe" is very palpable. This is 30 people in a room. Then, a year or two later, I read that the Beatles are onto TM and our little secret is being spread worldwide. Great. I still meditate.

Q: But the TM and Indian influence of 1967 still reverberates, and initially the calming effect informed your drum style. I know the Doors mixed theater, drama and psychedelic elements into the sound equation.

A: So maybe 1966, 1967, I was noticing in the traditional Indian ragas you gotta wait for your climax. It's not a quickie, you know. So that was the influence. Frankly, TM is the reason the Doors are together. TM. You could buy instant nirvana for $35 then. Now it's thousands of dollars. And TM glued together myself, Ray, Robby and Jim.

I don't know if you know this story. Jim didn't meditate, Robby and I went and Ray was there. That's where we met. One time, Jim came and he wanted to look into Maharishi's eyes... and Jim later said, "Well, he's got something. I'm not gonna meditate, but he's got something." This was the first class in the country. We were two years ahead of the Beatles, thank you. [Laughs.]

Ray had a previous relationship with World Pacific Records in 1965 when he was on the label with Rick and the Ravens and recorded for Dick Bock, who owned the label and released Ravi Shankar albums in the U.S. We got a couple hours of free studio time at World Pacific recording studios, and that's when we got to make a demo in 1965.

On the way into the studio Ravi Shankar is leaving with Alla Rakha, my idol, who I didn't know was going to be my idol yet, was on the way out with these little tabla drums, which I soon find out, by studying at the Kinnara School, are the most sophisticated drums in the world. I'm in awe of them. It's the East! And I'm just a surfer. Not literally, but from West L.A.

Robby and I went to Ravi Shankar's Kinnara School of Indian Music. When you're students at the Kinnara School of Music, you get to sit onstage with the master at UCLA's Royce Hall.

Later Robby and I go see Ravi play at the Hollywood Bowl, and George is on stage. Ravi didn't teach at the school, but he'd drop in and give a little lecture on "Sublimating Your Sexual Drive Into Your Instrument." Harrison was doing it in England. The whole Eastern Indian thing, Ravi Shankar, via George Harrison and the Beatles, saturated everything with paisley bedspreads soundwise. "The End" was a raga tune.

Later, George Harrison came to one of our recording sessions for *The Soft Parade*. You hear the Indian thing in techno stuff now. That came in and it was deep and it's still around. We need the East.

Q: In 1965, '66, and maybe through 1967, there was a sense of community and brotherhood in the local Hollywood psychedelic musical world and throughout the Summer of Love.

A: In May of 1966 the Doors were at the London Fog and I would go right up the street to the Whisky and hear Love play. Arthur Lee told Jac Holzman of Elektra Records about us when we played the Whisky. That was an incredibly sweet gesture, ya know. *Forever Changes* is a fuckin' masterpiece.

That's all I can fuckin' say, and it began in 1967. The first two albums they did in 1966 and '67 blew my mind. Here's this racially mixed group, not playing funk, playing electric folk. Ridiculous, with real tight pants! What!

During band rehearsals or just before we recorded, mainly I heard Jim's words live and by himself in the garage, or Ray would hand me a slip of paper and they were pulsating rhythms of words. Because Jim was a poet, they were edited. Like, "Break On Through" was so percussive. When we were recording and locked in, I was in it. We were just so in it. We were lost. Playing live, there were big sections on "The End," or "When the Music's Over," when we would vamp, and Jim would throw in anything. And then "Oh yeah? I'll throw that back at you. Check this out."

Q: What was happening in spring 1967?

A: May 20, on the same day we played the Whisky a Go Go in Hollywood, and the next night as well where we played with either the Byrds or Buffalo Springfield. "Break On Through" had got to number 11 when we played the Whisky, partially due to our phone calls. People were coming to the Whisky, like Sonny & Cher's management. Greene and Stone, the Turtles, Sunshine Company, the White Whale label people.

It was Greene and Stone who made the initial suggestion to cut down "Light My Fire" for radio since it was 6:50. Their suggestion was to put one half of the song on one side of a 45 and the rest on the flip side. That was cute. Subsequently, Robby and I went over to a local deejay's apartment, Dave Diamond from KBLA-AM, and he said it was a hit but mentioned, "You have to edit this down [for airplay]."

So, we pressed Paul Rothchild, and he just whacked at it, and all of us felt the cut was kinda brutal. But then we became the darlings of the FM radio stations who played the long version. And that jump-started the whole FM underground "We're cooler" scene. Which was very cool.

Q: May-August of that year, the Doors did concerts at the Earl Warren Showgrounds, Avalon Ballroom, Beverly Hills High School (Peters Auditorium), the Hullabaloo in Hollywood, Fillmore Auditorium, the Mount Tamalpais Outdoor Theater.

A: The Beverly Hills High School gym got psychedelicized! Actually it was the first time there was semi-Beatles hysteria. We played the middle of the gym and the audience was on the sides, we were the L.A. Lakers and people were screaming.

Q: You then performed up in San Francisco and out of California for the first time.

A: The Village Theater in New York, Steve Paul's Scene, and Town Hall in Philadelphia.

In San Francisco, first at the Avalon Ballroom, and then Fillmore Auditorium, where we kinda scared everybody.

"Light My Fire" hit No. 1 in July, our album went gold in September, and we did more gigs in Las Vegas, and the Cheetah in Venice.

Q: You played New York for the first time on June 11 at the Village Theater, and then a three-night engagement the 12th–15th at Steve Paul's The Scene.

I saw that 1968 Inglewood Forum concert where you had a horn and string session onstage for some numbers. I know the Doors initially wanted to have Johnny Cash on the show, but the promoter said no, because he was a felon. You then secured Jerry Lee Lewis because "he was acceptable." Morrison's voice was beautiful in that arena setting.

A: Jim had an astounding baritone. Unschooled. Never got nodes like Grace Slick and had to have surgery. God, if you don't have that bottom… It was luck. It was fate. He never sang before I saw him in the garage. It was kinda squeaky in the early days. He just was afraid to open up. How audacious. "OK. I've never sung and I'm gonna be the lead singer of a rock band."

Q: Yet, I know what kind of historic influence the Doors have had on culture and contemporary bands, let alone kick-starting psychedelic rock, but your work with the band in the Summer of Love gigs and your seminal albums also reminded me that the bands Cream, the Rolling Stones, and the Jimi Hendrix Experience all had jazz drummers playing rock 'n' roll.

A: That's right. That's good. I forget you're a drummer.
Ginger Baker. Cream's "Sunshine of Your Love" was out and we're in the studio, trying to play "Hello, I Love You," and we're in the studio, and Robby says, "Why don't you try and do that Cream beat where Baker sort of turns it around." And I did. Two bars of Ginger Baker is in "Hello, I Love You." [Laughs.] Ginger was in a trio with a lot of polyrhythm shit goin' on. Like Elvin. Charlie Watts's feel. He had the pocket. He got it from hearing all those jazz guys like Stan Levy and Chico Hamilton.
Mitch Mitchell's hands are really fast. More than Keith Moon. And Mitch is fluid as hell. I actually did "Little Wing"

on a Native American recording and did an instrumental version on a hand drum and still did Mitch's fills. A little tip of the hat.

Q: What was the best record you heard in 1967?

A: That sounds like a *MOJO* question. *Sgt Pepper's*. We were starting our second album, *Strange Days*, when our engineer Bruce Botnick got an advance copy of *Sgt. Pepper's* before it was released and played it for us. Oh, what a challenge… OK…

So, *Strange Days*, we were definitely more into experimental because of hearing that album, but we didn't want to do horns and strings, but it was so wild. Ringo did 400 pounds of overdubs on that album.

Q: In 2006 I attended a 35th-anniversary screening of George Harrison's *The Concert for Bangla Desh* in Burbank, California, at Warner Bros. Studio. Jim Keltner invited me. I spent 10 illuminating minutes with you and Ringo Starr. I had no idea about the drum-off competitions you described to us between University High School and Fairfax High School while Ringo was gigging at the Cavern in Liverpool. During our chat it was really apparent what a bond you have with Ringo.

A: I saw Ringo last year at the opening of the Beatles *LOVE* show in Las Vegas. I had to tell him how much I had admired the Beatles. His feel was it. People give him shit all the time. I don't know, but as one drummer to another, it felt real good to say, "Man, I just dug your feel."

We weren't in competition with the Beatles. When I think competition, it's sonic competition. Lennon and McCartney then were more semi-traditional songwriters, and we were West Coast acid heads. But sonically, we were challenged, and started to do backward piano tracks. "The recording studio is the fifth Door. Let's experiment." That's what *Sgt. Pepper's* did. We didn't try and copy Lennon and McCartney.

Q: What did the Summer of Love achieve?

A: 1967, we were naive, but felt, "We're changing the world." There were longhairs in every city, not in the Midwest so much, and thought we were taking over. And, actually, it was just seeds being planted which are blooming and will bloom a hundred years from now. Civil rights, feminism, peace movement, ecology, Native American rights, all that was planted. I remember poet Gary Snyder on a cable TV show, and they were trying to pin him down, "You're an ecological poet. You must be very depressed by the way the ecology environment is going and beaten up." He replied, "I'm not gonna buy that. Maybe it will be 200 years before big blooms come out from the seeds."

Jim Roup, 2018

I lived across the way from the Densmore family on Wilkins Avenue in Westwood. I was a friend of Jim Densmore, younger brother of John. I would hear John playing drums in 1962. I always loved seeing John's bass drum sitting by the door with a logo of his high school dance band that his mother Margaret designed. This was before John went to Valley State College.

In the summer of 1965, as the Doors were just developing their stage repertoire, my friend Steve Gordon, who was also a good friend of Jim Densmore, would lend albums to Jim for his brother's rock band of the time, including the Rolling Stones' *Out of Their Heads*.

In 1966 the Whisky a Go Go would have Sunday matinees and I would see on the marquee Love and Doors. In early 1967 I was inside Wallichs Music City and spotted the new Doors album with John Densmore, my old Westwood neighbor. A short while later I was on Sunset Strip one night and I recognized John Densmore wearing hippie garb with a gas can in his hand. So I went up to him. "Hi. I'm Jim Roup." "Oh, yes! My little brother's friend." He asked me, "Do you want to meet my band?" "Sure!"

We strolled down to the Whisky to Clark Street, where a nice car was waiting. Inside in the back seat were the three Doors crunched together. John introduced me to Ray, Robby and Jim. Ray and Robby were friendly. Jim kind of looked up, arms folded, and nodded.

On May 20, 1967, I was attending North Hollywood High School, and went with some friends to nearby Birmingham High School in Encino to see the Doors, Jefferson Airplane, Merry-Go-Round, the Nitty Gritty Dirt Band and the Peanut Butter Conspiracy, who were all on the football field. And a Mexican group called the Distortions participating in a Pepsi Battle of the Bands.

In September 1967, on the night the Doors were scheduled to appear on *The Ed Sullivan Show*, I was in Westwood and ran into Ray and Margaret Densmore taking a stroll.

I was at the Whisky on April 7, 1968, and saw Traffic at the Whisky. In line with us hippies was Peter Tork of the Monkees, looking very cool, but taking shit from some of the crowd about the Monkees not playing all the instruments on their first couple of albums. Buddy Miles was onstage with Traffic but didn't jam with them. The show ended, the crowd filed out, and I look around and notice Jim Morrison and Davy Jones of the Monkees having a friendly conversation on the corner of Clark and Sunset. Sugar Bear, a Sunset Boulevard fixture, was present, and Jim comically kicked him with his boot.

I was waiting for my dad to pick me up because it was a school night. And Jim was waiting for his ride. Out of the blue a Mustang car pulled up with four or five girls, and they proceed to yell obscenities at Jim and toss trash paper at him. In my 17-year-old mind I was a bit confused—"Is this how a rock star is treated?" Jim's driver arrived and so did mine.

On July 5, 1968, I bought a cheap seat and went to see the Doors, the Chambers Brothers, Steppenwolf and Sweetwater at the Hollywood Bowl and sat with my pal Marty. Happy to see the Doors headline this legendary venue. "Unknown Soldier" was very theatrical.

During 1968–1970 I saw Jim at the Whisky several times. One night he was acting goofy with some friends and taunting Mario, who ran the place, holding a can of beer. Mario said, "Jim, you gotta knock this drinking." Another time Jim was in front of me on the street with a woman on his arm slightly drunk, and then an hour later Jim was very sober speaking with doorman Albert.

In the very early '70s I once sang backup with Gene Vincent and played drums around the Southern California area, backing up the likes of Big Joe Turner, Dorsey Burnette, Ray Campi, Johnny Legend, and Davie Allen and the Arrows. I had a gig in Westlake Village at an Italian restaurant, and guitarist Dennis Coffey came by one night and jammed with us for an hour. Sometime in 1971 I was in Westwood one evening and went to the Glendon Theater for a midnight screening of *The T.A.M.I. Show* but without the Beach Boys segment. I was in line and there was Ray, Robby and John right in front of us.

Heather Harris, 2017

On December 23, 1967, I saw and took a photo of the Doors at Shrine Exposition Hall, downtown L.A., having begged a ride to same (then underage with no car, me, blasphemy for SoCal). I know because it says so on my envelope with the negatives of the crap camera of my teens. Aforementioned crap camera meant I had to position myself right next to the stage to capture anything usable. The leather trousers must have ripened without the benefit of much cleansing: Jim smelled bad. And that's all that is recalled. It was that sort of night in the '60s.

Jim Morrison at the Shrine Auditorium
Photo by Heather Harris

What was far more indelibly imprinted in the brain cells were Doors tales at UCLA when I matriculated, still freshly told from a mere few years' space. The film department knew exactly which lockers held the Doors' weed, and exactly which cheap Mexican restaurant was most frequented by Jim and Ray Manzarek (Pancho's Family Restaurant on Santa Monica Boulevard in West L.A., a bit of a misnomer. It was mainly a dive bar with a single table and two chairs, presumably for the titular family. Bonus feature: next door to Papa Bach (geddit?) Bookstore for après-dining literary browsing. Both establishments long gone in the Paisley Corridors of Time...)

Lastly were the three degrees of separation at my UCLA student dormitory, Weyburn Hall. My writer friend Suzanne R. and Jim Morrison, hot from their get-together at the 1970 Isle of Wight music festival, were frequently spotted together at the dorm, often playing pool in the rec room. Ah, the memories of college days and and nights!

Stephen J. Kalinich, 2015

Jim Morrison was a guy I loved. He loved Brian Wilson's music.

We were not great friends, but we knew each other, and he was always receptive, kind, and loved it when I recited for him and Pam.

Pam was his girlfriend. She had a little green VW Bug. It must have been 1966, '67 or '68. My memory is not clear. I had just signed with the Beach Boys' Brother Records.

I did not yet have a car. I was hitchhiking on Santa Monica Boulevard in the early afternoon, and a little green Bug pulled over and a sweet young girl, young woman picked me up. It was Pam. The Doors were not huge yet. The myth and the legend had not been formed. They were playing at the Whisky on Sunset almost every night. A few records out and they were hot to me but not like a worldwide phenomenon. We started talking and I recited to her and we spent a couple of hours together. She pulled the car over. I thought she was hot cute, but I did not flirt with her out of respect for Jim, who I

75

had not even met yet. She loved the poem and said Jim would love them.

She really liked the words to "Leaves of Grass," the one based on the Walt Whitman poem, my version of it. Everyone thought it was about marijuana, but it was not.

Carl Wilson produced this song. Anyway, a few days later she called and we got together with Jim. He was very kind, appreciative, really enjoyed the poems and the way I did them. He loved "The Magic Hand" and "If You Knew." Anyway, I had just signed with the Beach Boys and Brother Music as a writer and was getting very busy.

Alex Del Zoppo, 2017

1967 was a culturally transformative year, to say the least. San Francisco was the throbbing heart of rock music. But L.A. supplied the blood, as that's where the music business was. And L.A. was about to take the steering wheel again.

By 1967 I was back home in L.A. again, six months out of my active-duty stint with the United States Air Force Reserves, renewing my acquaintance with the real world and soaking in every fragment of the changes that had happened since I was gone, especially the revolutionary transformation that was taking place in the local music world.

A year earlier, I had come home on leave for 10 days, and was astounded by how much had changed in such a short period, but now, it was in a constant state of flux, shifting by the minute.

I found myself back at Los Angeles City College, studying music again, and playing nightly at the Scarab, a club/hang near the junior college with a jazz/Latin/classical jam band consisting of friends from school, which would soon morph into Sweetwater. We had different players each night, whichever JC instrumentalists would choose to show up on any given night, keeping things interesting, and keeping us on our toes, despite being swacked to the eyeballs. Life was mostly good... again.

In that era, we informed ourselves by word of mouth or by reading *The Los Angeles Free Press*. Glancing through that venerable rag, I began to become aware of a new band called the Doors, seeing their name pop up fairly often. And driving along the Sunset Strip to see one of my favorite acts, the Byrds, I also noticed the Doors on the Whisky's marquee. I thought to myself, "They must be a hardworking local band, 'cause they're always playing somewhere," piquing my curiosity.

But it wasn't until I was driving one sunny afternoon and the radio played "Light My Fire" that I first paid serious attention to them.

It had an undeniable groove, a palpable eerie sense that pervaded it in an inexplicable way, and an enthralling voice that was somehow both inviting and frightening, melding perfectly with the bizarre lyrics.

Moreover, barely a minute into it, they began a wild long-form jam, which held my attention from beginning to end. It was irresistible. The organ solo found its way through this frightening odal landscape, slowly building to a series of triplets, seemingly teasing the drummer with them, and him teasing back with his own, leading to an all-but-visible climax, followed by a respite that I fully expected to be the vocal coming back in again. But, they weren't done yet— then the guitar comes in with those brilliant jazz-blues hybrid licks and reaches his own climax before that spooky voice comes back in, with a different, more intense melody no less! Absolutely audacious! These guys could play!

In an understatement, they had my fucking attention.

When the FM DJ enthusiastically said, "That was a brand-new cut from the Doors," it was an "Aha!" moment for me! They had played all seven glorious minutes of it! I distinctly remember thinking to myself, "So that's what they sound like!" They were at once whimsical, musically astute, mysterious and with just enough darkness to intrigue me!

These "expanded solo sections" were what seemed to be in the air at the time, but not on the air. Bands in San Francisco had begun to explore lengthy instrumental excursions into uncharted musical waters when they played live, this during the end of the era of standard-issue 2:45 radio-ready singles.

And by the nature of what our band was, we had been doing that sort of free-form modal thing in our instrumental jam band every night at the Scarab. We had to: We had no singers, little material that any of those temporary band members could join in on, and many hours to fill nightly, so everything became fairly elastic. Amazingly, in the ensuing months, and in some totally unexpected ways, our two bands' paths would begin to cross.

One night, some months before that, while going about our instrumental jams, Albert Moore, playing his flute over a microphone, saw a young girl among the crowd. Oddly, she was singing while we played a minor-key jam based on a series of chords that I had come up with. She was singing out loud, loud enough for us to hear her, and it was something which seemed to fit what we were playing. While we continued to play, Albert beckoned her to the stage, and she came up and continued to sing, but now over his mic.

It turned out to be "Motherless Child," an old gospel standard, but it sounded completely different than any of us had ever heard it before. She sang a few verses with power, grace and confidence, and then jumped off the stage amid rousing applause from the audience, and disappeared into the crowd. It was a surprise to everyone in the place, including her! We, of course, continued to play that same jam for another 20 minutes or so, but when we took a break, we looked for her, and she was nowhere to be found.

A month or so later, after much searching and consternation, we finally got a lead on her. It turned out that

78

she was not an LACC student after all, but a 17-year-old high school girl from Glendale, who'd snuck out of her mom's house and hung around these kinds of places on occasion. Swallowing hard, we decided to think toward a positive future and asked her to join us.

I had a fairly different vision of what we could become with this new unexpected and powerful element, and soon pared down the band to keep some of the unique flavor, but add some balls to it, becoming a little less eclectic and a lot more electric.

We began rehearsals with a general goal in mind: Be so damn good, before we ever play in public, that we won't be denied. Businesswise, we were all fledglings, but we had a guru (and infrequent guitarist), Harvey Gerst, who had been in the music business all his life, in one capacity or another, and had co-written a couple of songs with Roger McGuinn for the Byrds.

He was also designing and developing a new music instrument amplifier company called Accoustic Control, with Steve Marks, and promised each of us would have one when the time was right. Besides being the nicest human we'd met in the music business, he helped and encouraged us tremendously, and instilled in us the vague notion that since the Doors had played the Whisky, and won a recording contract, that we might follow their path. But this was 1967, and things were changing.

During months of rehearsals, we began hearing about this odd thing called a "pop festival"—it was to be held in Monterey, California. As the time for it grew near, we convinced ourselves that we needed to go there, to see what it was all about. We drove up in two cars, and slept in them too, but awoke to experience the most glorious phenomenon that we could've ever imagined: live rock music, played outdoors among thousands of peaceful fans.

We came back to L.A. with a different goal: to be a part of that, and play those kinds of gigs! We told Harvey our new goal, and in his lovable way, he immediately said, "OK, No problem!" Through his connections, he got us an audition to play at a love-in, which was essentially, a Pop Fest without pay.

It must sound like a joke to read that we had to audition for a free gig, but we were virtually unknown, and this was a special one, with some major names on the bill, Iron Butterfly and Phil Ochs. Additionally, it was sponsored by an L.A. radio station and MC'd by Elliot Mintz. Here, we played our very first gig before thousands of young people, but we were more than ready. After we played, Elliot asked us if we had representation. Sensing that we didn't know what that meant, he continued, "A manager or agent. If not, there's a fellow here that would like to talk to you about that."

And eventually, through this connection and a series of happy accidents, we were led to Bruce Glatman, who became our manager. Bruce began to get us gigs that same week—fun and prestigious ones too, like the Artists and Models Ball. We began to play regularly in and around California.

Soon, we were playing the Whisky, often for weeks at a time, routinely opening for major acts, and ironically, we eventually got signed by Warner Bros., after Mo Ostin saw us there while opening for Janis Joplin with Big Brother and the Holding Company.

He was fairly new to the business but seemed to know nearly everyone in it, and amazingly, one of them was Asher Dan, who was involved with the Doors management team. So we began to open for the Doors too, but at increasingly larger venues, such as the Shrine Auditorium and the Forum. This seemed to be a good fit, as both acts' sound was heavily dependent on keyboards (we had no guitarist for 95 percent of our three-and-a-half-year run).

The Shrine Concert Hall in downtown L.A. was a massive box, and the stage was built higher off the floor than at most venues. After we had done our set, and it was time for the Doors to play, Ray, Robby and John assembled onstage. The stage remained dark, as always, between acts. After waiting for what seemed like 15 minutes, while the band was already onstage, adjusting their settings, Jim was not to be seen. At the time, it began to feel as if he may not come up at all, and the audience grew restless. An envoy from backstage came up and told the instrumentalists to begin to play.

Eventually, a couple of their roadies had to practically carry Jim up from the dressing room backstage to his mic, where he grasped onto the stand, holding on for dear life as if it were a walker. While the instrumentalists continued to comp that rhythmic groove, he stood still and silent in his dark leather pants, for an interminable amount of time, before he began to sing. When he finally sang, it was barely sufficient, not nearly as good as we knew it could be. The stage lights were still not turned on until a while after that, for some reason. The audience didn't seem to know the difference, about any of that, or didn't care. They seemed to get wound up when he began to sing. But it took several songs for him to actually be an equal part of that great band.

As I watched, mesmerized, from stage right, standing just feet behind Manzarek, I began to pay less attention to Jim, and more to Ray. He played not only his incredibly demanding organ parts, but the bass parts as well, on a Fender Rhodes Bass keyboard. His hands seemed to each have a distinct mission, the left holding the bass groove tightly together while doing mind-blowing things on the organ with his right.

Of course, many traditional organ players play a bass part with a slightly different organ sound, but to his credit, he played this instrument with the feel that an actual bass player would, and with his impeccable touch, we didn't miss having an electric bass guitar at all. Together with the rock-steady Robby and John, they tore up that giant hall, smokin' musicians that they were. And I know that it's not my imagination that they did "Light Fire" way longer than the record! Just gorgeous.

Having grown familiar with their recordings by then, I already thought highly of them as a band. They were uniquely inventive, solid instrumentalists who played with feeling and excitement, and Jim's voice was mesmerizing. But while watching them perform live that night, especially from so close a vantage point, I noticed that while the instrumentalists were always uncannily attuned to one another, Morrison seemed detached, nearly feral at times.

Being the cynical bastard that I was, I wondered if this was a cultivated act, a ruse of sorts? Word from the road managers was that it was assuredly not fake and, in fact, that he was fortunate to be standing (mostly) upright that night. Being aware of the available drugs of that era, I could only guess what would render him so distant.

When we played with them at the Forum in Inglewood, California, a much more massive and elegant venue, things were a lot different. The bill was the Doors, Sweetwater, and Jerry Lee Lewis—in that order. Again, all keyboard-heavy acts. However, someone decided that another solo act should also be on the bill—well after all the advertising, posters and billboards had it locked in. Additionally, being a special gig for them, they added orchestral players and an electric bass guitar to accompany them. Consequently, when we arrived, our roadies told us that "everything is going to have to happen quicker tonight—that means you'll be going on soon, and possibly do a shorter set because they'll need time to set up these extra players."

As it turns out, a solo Asian-string instrumentalist was now to play as well. That meant that our set definitely was going to be cut shorter, after Jerry's. But even that was not how things turned out.

We got word that Jerry Lee was "stuck in traffic," and that Sweetwater would have to go on before him—out of order. But this was an important gig for us too! We didn't want to relinquish that choice spot on the bill. We waited as long as we could, until it was a choice of playing as the opening band, or not at all. Bruce was not in town to fight this particular boondoggle for us... so we eventually gave in and went on before Jerry—at first, with the fucking lights on! Jerry Lee conveniently showed up after we were through. We'd been had—he skunked us. We had become road veterans by then, and most things didn't bother us, but that didn't go down well. Jim seemed a lot more settled down at this gig, and it sounded much more like the records, especially with the string players, but we were too pissed to hang around for very long.

Shortly following that, we stopped by the Doors office, upstairs on Santa Monica Boulevard and La Cienega in WeHo, for some business, as we had begun to share roadies. While there, I asked if they had any posters left from the Forum gig. They were sparse and iconic with a graphic of a large lizard in the center. Vince Traynor, their road manager, said they were all out but that there was one on a telephone pole out on the street nearly at the bottom of their stairs. As it turned out, it was a large, single "printer's proof sheet," combining several Doors/Sweetwater Forum flyers and a few Chambers Brothers ones. I took it, because I wanted to have a souvenir of that gig. Ironically, after many decades, that turned out to be quite valuable, being the exceedingly rare item that it was.

I marvel now, looking back after all those years, at how heady and wacky those days were, and also how people we met continued to intersect with one another, often in bizarrely unexpected ways. One afternoon while we were between gigs, our old guru, Harvey Gerst, called to tell us that Vince Traynor called him, asking to "round up as many Acoustic Control amplifiers that were in L.A. for a Doors show at the Hollywood Bowl."

We, along with several L.A. acts (because nearly every major act was addicted to the great sound projection those amps had) readily agreed to let them use our amps on loan. I went up to the Bowl with our roadie, Steve Doyle, who used to work for the Doors under Vince, and checked out the amazing spectacle. A virtual wall of sound!

In that setting, their performance seemed spectacular, and it wasn't just the wall of amps or the setting. From the beginning, despite some mic problems, everyone was at their best. The band was amazing for that gig, and Jim seemed relaxed and was really spot-on for those performances. From the slowly building excitement for the opening of "When the Music's Over," they rocked the hills!

Their unique version of "Back Door Man" was hard-hitting as always and completely satisfying. "Moonlight Drive" felt positively right with the audience being under the stars. I was backstage, but it felt magical, even from the wings. They built their way to a couple of encores. The inevitable "Light My Fire" certainly did just that to the audience, and was different than on record or any of the other times I'd witnessed them live. The jam part was still spellbinding, just a bit unique. When they reached those massive climaxes, everyone got off! The entire audience was in sync with them! Jim sang it a bit differently too—his melody was more tame, yet somehow more exaggerated, yet with the same spookiness that got me hooked the first time I'd heard it. And "The End" was positively explosive! A perfect way to end any set!

Jim seemed comfortable there, as if they were casually playing just another gig at the Whisky. More important, he was attentive to the band members throughout the night, adding occasional, obviously rehearsed theatrics, even dancing vigorously at times, and the crowd loved every minute of it. I did too!

Bless his troubled soul. And bless Ray Manzarek. They will live forever.

The Doors, **Marina Muhlfriedel,** April 19, 2017

It's a sticky September morning. 1967. I clutch my journal and a bag of red and black licorice twists I share with a friend. The sky is bellicose brown, the air so thick with smog I detect a dusting of petroleum on the licorice. We wait outside of Rancho Music on Pico in West Los Angeles. About 20 of us, most ditching school, are in line, itching to get our hands on *Strange Days*, the Doors new album.

It's 10 a.m. and we know we need to be there. It won't be the last time either. There is an unspoken loyalty toward the Doors. They are like us, only more so—a resonance of the desolate West in the belly of a crowded belligerent city. Purposely wading into strange. Exalting the ancient reptilian pulse that has always lurked beneath the sun-kissed façade we call home. This is not spit, shine and put on a show. This is real.

The Doors at the Hollywood Bowl, July 5th, 1968
Photo by Henry Diltz

Our mothers and our aunties had Frank Sinatra and Tony Bennett to swoon over. Our older cousins fell for Elvis and Frankie Valli; even we had Brit cuteness like Paul McCartney and Donovan to crush on. But the Doors were different. Jim Morrison was different. He was our first real live bad boy. Dangerous. Passionate. Seductive. Untamed. We were in love and maybe a bit scared. There were rumors of anger and violence, but we shrugged them off as flaws in his anguished poet soul.

Oh, and that voice, that boisterous beauty, welling up from his volcanic shadowy soul. Taunting, sexual, surreal, serious—Jim Morrison was a high priest at a dark mass of his own design and imbued, like us, with a timeless sense of California.

Not far from Elektra Records on La Cienega I meet a guy who says he works at the Doors' nearby rehearsal studio. He tells me Jim kicked his girlfriend down the steps of their rented home, flung a beer bottle at a roadie. Tells me I can hang if I want, maybe Jim will be by later. I shrug; leave. I have homework.

My friend Bob reminds me that we walk the six miles from Beverlywood to the Hollywood Bowl to see the Doors in 1968. I think we hitchhike part of the way. The Chambers Brothers and Steppenwolf share the bill. I'm happy for the hits, but have no attachment to the bands. We're here for the Doors, and as soon as Ray Manzarek's organ starts to slink through the Bowl, we bolt from our seats and sneak down, closer to the stage for a better view.

The first two bars of "When the Music's Over" grab me by the wrist and pull me in. I connect to something I don't think anyone else can see. The dart of Jim's eyes, a momentary flaring of his hands. I feel his impatience, his not quite fitting the confines of his skin, his teetering on a line he's not sure we're ready to cross. The rest of the band tries to psychically, musically rein him in. Tether him to the moment.

But that isn't who Jim is. I can see it. I know it. The vocals stride on a high wire above the instrumentation, pretending to waver, then adroitly bound ahead, daring the music to keep pace with the Lizard King. But the lights are too bright; Jim and his vocals start to slip from the wire. Anger wells up, he threatens to throw us all down the steps of the rented house. He shifts palpably, dimensionally, takes a face from an ancient gallery and swings back up on the wire. Riveted. Real.

After "The End" Bob, another friend and I float all the way down Sunset Boulevard, buzzed on adrenaline. I get home late. Quiet as I can, I put the first Doors album on the RCA console in the living room, lie down and, still chewing a bit of Eden's apple, fall asleep dreaming that I'll never be the same again.

DOORS LIVE AT THE BOWL '68
RecordCollectorNews.com, 2012

LIVE AT THE BOWL, a Doors 1968 concert from the Hollywood Bowl, was just released on DVD, Blu-ray, and Digital Video from Eagle Rock Entertainment. A CD, Digital Audio, and double LP from the event was issued from Rhino.

The performance has been restored from original camera negatives and remixed and mastered using original multi-track tapes.

This Doors concert from July 5, 1968, is considered to be the band's finest documentation on film. The group's engineer Bruce Botnick has done a masterful job in this new restoration and an upgrade from previous video, DVD and laserdisc formats that have documented this regional experience.

"You can hear it as if you were at the Hollywood Bowl, onstage with us," states Ray Manzarek, who was joined

Jim Morrison at the Hollywood Bowl, July 5, 1968
Photo by Henry Diltz

88

at the legendary venue by John Densmore, Robby Krieger and Jim Morrison.

LIVE AT THE BOWL '68 includes three previously unreleased tracks from the performance. Technical issues with the recording of "Hello, I Love You," "The WASP (Texas Radio and the Big Beat)" and "Spanish Caravan" prevented them from being released in the past. Now, through meticulous restoration of the audio, all three are housed, marking the first time the concert has been available in its entirety.

LIVE AT THE BOWL '68—the definitive version of this concert—is available in several formats.

The DVD, Blu-ray and digital video each feature a 16x9 high-definition digital transfer with both a stereo and 5.1 audio soundtrack as well as over an hour of bonus material. Integrated in the additional content are *Echoes from the Bowl*, the Doors' route to the Hollywood Bowl; "You Had to Be There," memories of the Doors' performance at the Bowl; "Reworking the Doors," an in-depth look at how the film was restored; and three bonus performances: "Wild Child" from *The Smothers Brothers Comedy Hour* in 1968, "Light My Fire" from *The Jonathan Winters Show* in December 1967 and a version of Van Morrison's "Gloria" with specially created visuals.

"As far as the Hollywood Bowl, it was amazing to be asked to play the Bowl," offered Robby Krieger via email. "Growing up in Los Angeles and playing the Bowl must be like playing baseball in New York and playing Yankee Stadium. We were really psyched! So much so that we actually rehearsed! (first time ever just for a gig) and we decided to capture the whole thing on film (and 8-track tape) normally, we would just wing it at gigs... We might discuss what to start with, 2 or three songs and then just go with the flow.

"Looking back," added Krieger, "the rehearsal may have been a mistake. I think it may have made things a bit unspontaneous, not a good thing when the Doors were supposed to be so wild and free, never knowing what might happen next..... Also the fact that Jim was peaking on acid was not in line with such a tightly controlled show... Check out the Granada film, *Doors Are Open...* That was more of a spontaneous Doors show... Luckily, the footage from the Bowl looks great and we fixed up the missing songs, so we now have the complete show."

Geoff Kempin, executive producer for Eagle Rock, stated: "The Doors were one of THE most incredible live bands ever—we wanted to apply the top technology so that everyone can fully appreciate the phenomenon of the Doors captured at their height on 5 July 1968."

Paul Kantner, 2012

By the time Jefferson Airplane did the Monterey International Pop festival, we had a record deal with RCA and an album out that we recorded in Hollywood. As far as San Francisco being suspect of L.A. and Hollywood people, we always tried to get above that if possible as a general rule. People didn't like the Doors. 'Cause they were from L.A. [Laughs.] So there's an immediate antipathy, and I liked the Doors a lot and toured with them. I created that lack of that antipathy in myself. I rejected the suspicions of L.A. as a general rule. I thoroughly enjoyed L.A. and New York. I could make myself comfortable in either one of those cities. I liked San Francisco a lot.

Marty Balin interview, 2017
Record Collector News magazine

Q: Tell me about the Matrix club.

A: I opened the Matrix club in 1965 in San Francisco. Booked bands in 1966 and '67.

Q: The Doors played the Matrix club in very early 1967. I know in '67 and 1968 you toured the U.S. and Europe together.

A: I didn't see the Doors at the Matrix club but saw them many times. We worked and played with them many times in 1967 and '68. We did some high school and college shows together and toured Europe.

"I loved the Doors. Oh my God! I thought Jim Morrison was fantastic. I fortunately became a friend and hung out and got to drink with him. He'd read me his poems all the time. I thought that was funny. I thought Jim was great as an artist. Who knows? He would have probably gone into film and done movies. The guy was a good lookin' dude, man. I'd go out with him and try and pick up chicks and I was like invisible.

Grace Slick Interview, 2002

I interviewed Grace Slick after she published her autobiography *Somebody to Love?* A portion of our conversation was originally intended for *HITS* magazine. Due to space limitations it didn't appear, and it was published in my *This Is Rebel Music* book.

In our chat, Grace gleefully chronicles a sexual escapade with Jim Morrison during the 1968 Doors and Jefferson Airplane European tour, and happily admits she was the perpetrator knocking on his hotel room door.

Q: I liked your description of Jim as a floating art form with eyes who studied you and documenting a fruit-lubricated horizontal encounter with him.

A: There's a section in my book on Jim Morrison and, to this day, I still don't know what country we were in when I discuss it in the chapter, *Strawberry Fuck.*

I had to call [Doors manager] Danny Sugerman and ask him, "Could you possibly figure out where we would have been when I fucked Jim?"

To this day, I still don't know what country it was in.

He can be with you and not with you at the same time. And it's not the same as someone being snobby and mean and being detached. It's more like he has two things going on.

One, he's interacting with you and the world and whatever is going on around him. And two, you can see him enjoying what is also happening in his mind. Which may or may not have to do with what is going down at the moment.

So yes, I had sex with his mind, as well as his personality and every other thing I can think of.

Onstage he did what he wanted. So that's kinda doing what you want, rather than being an entertainer. More than an entertainer, Morrison just did what he felt at the time, and it may not have been what you want either. Or it may not have been what the band wanted. I'm sure, like me, when you can't count on what they're gonna do. That was kind of interesting. [Laughs.]

Carlos Santana Interview, 2017
Record Collector News magazine 2017

Q: Your autobiography *The Universal Tone: Bringing My Story to Light* really details the impact the new 1967 FM underground rock radio had on you in San Francisco.

A: It blew my mind when I found KSAN-FM radio station. They played the whole songs of Vanilla Fudge, Country Joe & the Fish, the long version of Traffic's "Smiling Phases," the long version of "Light My Fire." "Wow. This is really, really cool." Taking LSD and listening to Frank Zappa.

I'm very grateful that my timing with my mom and dad was perfect in being in San Francisco when it all hit: the

Doors, Grateful Dead, Ravi Shankar. Coltrane. There was an explosion of consciousness that made you question authority. Black power, rainbow power.

The only thing the Santana band never wanted to do was succumb to phony. We were watching what was all unfolding with Sly Stone and Jim Morrison and it was becoming too much for all of them. Becoming victims of an avalanche of illusion by not being prepared mentality to not deal with mass quantity adulation. I'm not dependent or addicted to mass adulation. That stuff makes me feel uncomfortable. I'm not afraid of it. I have learned to balance it.

Jan Alan Henderson, 2015
BRIEF ENCOUNTERS WITH THE LIZARD KING

Growing up in the '60s above the Sunset Strip was an experience that defies description. In those days, everything was possible; the world of music had just turned the real world upside down.

From 1965 to 1970, the Sunset Strip was my nocturnal home. I remember seeing Ray Manzarek, Robby Krieger, John Densmore, and the late Jim Morrison at the Whisky a Go Go before their first record came out. At that time, music was basically tribal dance music, but that night my 15-year-old world was turned inside out, and I was led to the Doors of Perception. The band I saw in my head from the sidewalk that night had a depth and presence that had never been seen in rock & roll.

I remember walking into Gazzarri's midway through one of the Doors' sets, and then a year later witnessed the phenomenon that the band had become one magical evening at the Hollywood Bowl. But none of this prepared me for my next encounter with the Doors—or I should say, A Door.

The summer of 1969 I walked into Sunset Sound looking for a job. The first person I saw at the studio was a guy named Brad Pinkstaff. He was an apprentice engineer, the job I had hoped to get. We became fast friends, and I became his unpaid assistant, and worked on projects with him—*Lord Sutch and His Heavy Friends*, to name one.

One day I walked into the Sunset Sound complex and someone said to me, "We need a vocal mic in Studio No. 2." So I went in and set up the mic, and walked out to the open-air foyer. There, waiting for his call to put vocal tracks down, was Jim Morrison, with a gallon bottle of Red Mountain wine; a vocal overdub for *Morrison Hotel*. Now, I had heard of Jim's antics, but this afternoon the Lizard King was nowhere to be found. Instead, I sat with Jim, had a Styrofoam glass of his wine, and talked about everyday things. He wanted to know about where I went to school and what my plans were. When I left the studio a short time later and walked down Sunset Boulevard, my feet weren't touching the ground, let alone the earth.

Somewhere in the span of the next 12 months, I was once again car-less. I was standing at the intersection of Lookout Mountain and Laurel Canyon with my thumb outstretched over the curb, below the traffic light. An American-built muscle car pulled up at the red light. "Get in," were the magic words as I slid in the passenger side and the light turned green. The driver was full-bearded and resembled a Northern California mountain man. I didn't know this guy from Adam, but it was his voice that caught my ear.

Then it hit me. I was sitting next to Jim Morrison. Not the Jim Morrison who mesmerized us at the Hollywood Bowl in July of 1968, when we pulled our usual admission stunt. (We'd walk to the end of Primrose Avenue off Outpost Drive, and crawl down the hillside and drop down to the back rows of the Bowl, blending in and taking whatever empty seats were available, steadily moving forward in the historic venue.) As he drove toward Mulholland Drive, I wondered what the future held for both of us. Little did we know that the Lizard King's time on the third stone from the sun was limited!

Bill Mumy, 2017

The day before Neil Armstrong walked on the moon, I was at the Aquarius Theatre with my Barnes and Barnes partner, Robert Haimer, seeing the Doors. We attended the early show and we got there early and secured seats in the very front row. The gig was great.

Morrison was focused and low-key, but he was a mighty force. I thought he looked great. Thick beard, Mexican peasant shirt and orange Aviator sunglasses. Ray wore a white T-shirt. I took several photographs during the gig and have one of the few pics of Morrison onstage looking directly into a camera lens.

"Celebration of the Lizard," "You Make Me Real" and "Soul Kitchen" were highlights for me. The Doors were such a unique band. To this day, I appreciate Morrison's poetry and lyrics. He was a genuine artist. They all were great and had musical styles that were/are instantly recognizable.

I consider myself fortunate to have been there.

Gene Aguilera, 2017

As an inquisitive teenager with a wandering mind, I used to love to look through the *Los Angeles Free Press*, the infamous, radical, underground newspaper of the '60s. One day, there it was: a small ad saying the Doors were coming to the Aquarius Theatre on July 21, 1969! Elektra Records, the Doors' label, had begun a policy of renting the venue on Monday nights (this being the dark night of the play *Hair*) to showcase their roster. Naturally, I had to go, but was without wheels at that point; so after much begging (my 16th birthday was coming soon), my aunt, Julie Gillis, agreed to take me and my two cousins to see one of my favorite bands.

As we departed East L.A., making our way toward the Sunset Strip, my aunt Julie began to worry about taking her 11-year-old daughter, Debbie, with us. Just a few months earlier in Miami, the Doors' lead singer Jim Morrison had been arrested for indecent exposure onstage. She said, "What if he takes it out again? I don't want Debbie to see any of this." But it didn't matter to me, there was *no* other place in the world I would rather be.

With its painted psychedelic exterior and an exquisite art-deco interior, we had arrived at the Aquarius Theatre and sat about halfway up from the stage. With the band still reeling from the Miami bust, an aura of danger lurked thick in the air; when suddenly to the stage strolls a dwarf (adding to the circus-like atmosphere), named Sugar Bear, to announce the band, "Ladies and Gentlemen... the Doors!" We were now ready for the Lizard King.

Jim Morrison looked so much different in person than the album covers I had studied; he arrived with sunglasses, a thick beard, and a paunch around his waist. But for this hometown "live" recording (resulting in tracks for the *Absolutely Live* LP), Morrison introduced an edgy new trick to his usual theatrical drama. With the spotlight on, Morrison appeared incredulously high up in the rafters, grabbed a rope and swung to the stage, Tarzan-style, leaving the entire crowd gasping at what they saw.

My aunt Julie had her coat ready to cover Debbie's eyes (if Jim was going to whip it out, as he did in Miami), but that never happened, thank God, Morrison instead throwing Styrofoam balls out to the crowd. In my youthful excitement, I ran toward the stage and caught a few. A pretty hippie girl next to me was disappointed at not catching anything, so I gave her one, and in turn, she gave me a great big kiss; witnessed by all my group. This was the dawning of the age of Aquarius.

Burton Cummings, 2016
Courtesy of Burton Cummings

It was a night in 1969… it was the first time in my life that I had ever set foot on California soil. The Guess Who were in Los Angeles, I believe, to appear on *American Bandstand.* We had already had "These Eyes," and I think "Laughing / Undun" had been released, but the dates are a bit fuzzy.

We came into town from the airport and checked in to the Travel Lodge on Sunset, right near La Brea, at about nine in the evening. I had never seen L.A. before. I was enthralled…

I wanted to go out sightseeing, but the other three guys were just not interested.

Since being a small kid in the north end of Winnipeg, I had been a huge fan of *77 Sunset Strip.* Saw every single episode. One of my heroes had been Edd "Kookie" Byrnes. He parked the cars at Dino's Lounge on Sunset. That was the first thing I wanted to see.

So I left the hotel alone and walked west on Sunset, toward the ocean. It's a pretty fair hike from La Brea to where Dino's used to be, but I walked briskly and before I knew it, there I was, standing on the hallowed ground of Dino's parking lot. That fantasy being fulfilled, I continued west on Sunset toward the Whisky a Go Go. I just had to see the place that had housed such bands as the Doors, the Byrds, Buffalo Springfield and a host of others.

Finally got there about half past midnight. Whatever band had played that night was already finished… most of the remaining crowd was either drunk or pretty buzzed on something. Eric Burdon was there over in a corner, slouched behind a table with some friends. I drank in the vibes for about 10 minutes, milling over in my mind the countless golden moments in pop music that had occurred in the tiny club.

About one in the morning I decided I'd had my fun and left the Whisky to hail a cab back to my hotel. Right outside the front door on Sunset there were about three or four cabs, very unusual for Los Angeles. I jumped into one and before I could say "I'm going back down Sunset to the Travel Lodge at La Brea," the cab driver said, "So… I guess you're going to the big party too…"

Well, I'm not a complete fool, so I replied, "Yeah."

So now here I am, been in Los Angeles for a total of about four hours in my entire life, and I'm on my way to the "big party" up in the Hills. We started to wind up the roads of the Hollywood Hills. Ten minutes into this cab ride I decided to come clean with the driver. I told him that I wasn't really invited to the "big party," but if he'd take me there, I'd pay my fare, and then maybe he could wait and see if I got in. He agreed.

We finally arrived at a house that looked like the *Beverly Hillbillies* mansion. I got out, paid the driver and told him to wait for me if I didn't manage to get in.

I rang the doorbell of the huge front door and some loon opened it and shouted, "Come on in…"

So much for the cab driver waiting… there was no need for that now.

The scene was insane… naked people in the pool, people swilling liquor and snorting coke everywhere, and just noise, noise, noise. I had been in California for a total of about four hours, and here I was at some wingding up in the Hollywood Hills. Some guy with a British accent told me to follow him to the kitchen for a beer, which I did quite willingly. So… now I at least had a beer.

I walked around, kind of intimidated, not knowing a soul in the house. There was a small, cutoff upright piano in the corner of the main living room, so I sat down on the bench, put my beer down and started tinkering softly, down in the range of middle C. No one could hear me anyway, so this went on for about 10 minutes.

Very unobtrusively, someone sat down next to me on the piano bench, and started tinkering softly on the upper register beside me. I didn't look up for a few minutes, but when I did, I thought this guy looked kinda familiar... another glance, and sure enough, it was Jim Morrison... black jeans, dark brown suede bomber jacket, full beard and lots of hair... classic Jimbo...

No one else in the room seemed to know it was him... either that or they were entirely uninterested.

I swilled the rest of my beer and asked him if he wanted one... you see, by now, I knew where the beers were. Jim followed me to the fridge in the kitchen and we grabbed two cold ones. Now... this was not long after Jim's trouble in Miami. The Doors hadn't performed in a while, and I think the trial was still pending. I didn't want to get in his face, but I had to ask him "So, man, what about Miami... a lot of shit? What's happening?"

He just grinned one of those fabulous "Jimbo grins" and said, "Oh, it'll be all right..."

We both went back to the piano bench, but this time we just sat down and drank our beers. About this time, two young Hollywood strumpet types came up to Jim and said, "It's time to go, Jim..." He pulled some keys out of his pocket and started to make his way to the front door. He'd had a few and I thought he shouldn't be driving. Out of the fucking blue I just said, "Hey man, don't drive... let me drive... I'll take you where you want to go, and you can drop me off there... I'll get back home later..."

To my amazement, he handed me the keys and said, "OK, let's go."

The two girls led Jimbo to his car (at least I assumed it was his)... it was a shiny silver GTO with a black vinyl roof. He opened the trunk to reveal a huge aluminum washtub filled with iced Miller High Life beers. He and the girls grabbed one apiece and the three of them climbed into the back seat. I got behind the wheel and started to drive.

Now the last thing Jim had to hear at this point was that I was the biggest Doors freak in North America and that I knew everything about him. He had no idea what all this was meaning to me, but I never even let on that I was a musician. Silence for a while… Jim would occasionally say, "Turn right here" or "Just keep going down this street"… I had no idea in hell where I was driving, and I was new to L.A. and there was liquor in the car, so I just drove cautiously like a limo driver. Once in a while Jim would say to one of the girls, "Some for the driver, some for the driver," upon which one of the girls would hand me one of the beers so I could down a sip.

After a while the conversation started.

My god, he was articulate… even half drunk, he was more lucid and intelligent than 90 percent of all the people I've ever met in this lifetime.

He was so well read… he talked about great authors… Mark Twain, Rudyard Kipling, Lewis Carroll and many others I can't recall now. He talked about the universe and its size… he talked about the great painters of the Renaissance era… he talked about great poets, touching from time to time on William Blake and maybe Baudelaire… I'm recalling whatever I can remember after all these years…

Every time their bottles were empty, I was told to pull over and stop, whereupon one of the girls would get out and bring in another few Miller High Lifes from the trunk. This went on for hours. The three of them were getting drunker and friendlier in the back seat…

It was all so surreal… my first night ever in Los Angeles, and I was chauffeuring the Lizard King around on his turf. Just about sunrise, the three of them suddenly said that they "had to get back to their place," whatever that meant. I just said, "OK, I'll get out here... Jim, let one of the girls drive." I got out of the GTO on Ventura Boulevard. In the valley, one of the girls got behind the wheel, and I watched the GTO pull away westward on Ventura... and that was that.

I didn't have much money in my pocket, and I had to take a combination of buses and a cab to get back to our Travel Lodge hotel. Hell, I'd ended up on the other side of the hill. I was a long, long way from Bachman, Peterson, and Kale...

When I finally got back to the Travel Lodge, the sun was up... it was the next morning. What had happened to me hadn't really sunk in yet. I told the whole story to the other three that morning. I don't think Kale and Peterson believed me for a second. I think Randy believed me, but he didn't say much. The Doors had never really meant much to the other guys. I was younger, and I had done acid, so the gap between myself and the other three was enormous at that particular point in time.

Just over a year later, Jim Morrison was gone... forever...

Years later, I became part of a weekly bunch of NBA fanatics who would all get together on Sundays to watch Michael Jordan on television whenever we got the chance. One of this group was Ray Manzarek. When I told him about my night with Jim, he told me, "Hell, man, you spent more time with Jim than almost anybody."

To this day, I feel it was the music gods giving me a small gift to reward my fascination with music in general, in particular the Doors and Jim's work. It was a night to remember... and I will remember it always...

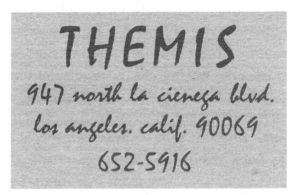

THEMIS
947 north la cienega blvd.
los angeles. calif. 90069
652-5916

Themis card courtesy of Anne Moore

Rob Hill, 2017

In the fall/winter of 1969, just six months after Jim's arrest in Miami, Pamela plunked down $75K of Jim's royalty check from *Strange Days* on a tiny showroom on the trendy art gallery row of La Cienega Boulevard, just a few blocks away from the Doors' offices, and the couple's apartment on West Norton Avenue. One drunken night before opening the boutique Jim decided the place should be called "Fucking Great," but when more sober minds came around they settled on Themis, the name of the Greek goddess of divine order, law and custom.

Pam immediately went on a first-class buying spree in North Africa, the Middle East, India, Paris, and London, scooping up rare silk blouses, ruby embroidered vests, funky tapestries, fur shawls, and enough peacock feathers to blanket most of the walls and mirrored ceiling. Themis was filled with perfumed candles, incense and dozens of stuffed animals: unicorns, monkeys and tigers… but not much else. There were no real hours for the shop and oftentimes it was only one-third full of clothes. (Reportedly, just a few days before actress Sharon Tate was killed in the Manson murders, she stopped by the shop at midnight and spent a small fortune on blouses and skirts.) One thing it was full of, however, were Pamela's flunky friends, who hung out and partied at all hours of the night.

In the one infamous photo shoot that Raeanne Rubenstein did for *SHOW* magazine, Jim and Pam, fresh and relaxed, can be seen horsing around and posing with a colorful motley crew of '60s hangers-on, including good friend and fashion designer/writer Tere Tereba. When Pamela was in the shop, she was to be called Pamela Roselilly, her "professional" name.

In short order, however, the shop had gone through almost $300K of Jim's money. And in the spring of 1971, the doomed rock 'n' roll couple fled to Paris. Reportedly, when Pamela returned from Paris in the summer of 1971, after Jim's death, she marched into Themis one day and doused perfume over all of the clothing. Themis closed soon thereafter.

Rodney Bingenheimer, 2017

I was writing a music column for *GO!* magazine and was invited to the festival. I knew the Doors. I saw them play in 1967 in Northridge at the Fantasy Faire in July of 1967. Jefferson Airplane were there, along with the Iron Butterfly, Fraternity of Man, Grass Roots, and the Kaleidoscope. A bunch of acts. I also went to see the Doors in San Jose.

I hung out a bit with them at Elektra studios one time on La Cienega when Kim Fowley was producing an album on Gene Vincent. Skip Battin was there. And the Doors were in the next studio and popped in to say hello. The Doors were really nice people.

In 1968 when I was first writing for *GO!* I covered the opening of the rock 'n' roll movie *Privilege* that starred Paul Jones, who had been the lead singer of Manfred Mann. Jean Shrimpton was in the film, too. Jim Morrison was at the premiere. Also in the room were Mick Jagger, Arthur Lee and Sky Saxon. And some of the Iron Butterfly. All the lead singers sitting together in a couple of rows checking out this rock 'n' roll movie where the lead singer is like a religious figure.

I'd see Jim around town, ran into him at the Copper Penny restaurant in Hollywood, which is now Denny's. One night Jim was drunk outside the Whisky a Go Go and sitting on the curb. A friend and I drove him up to where Eric Burdon was staying in Bel-Air.

In 1969 I saw Jim do his poetry reading on Sunset Strip. Other poets were on the event. Kim Fowley was there. His driver at the time was Warren Zevon. I also saw a couple of the Aquarius Theatre shows by the Doors in 1969. They were great. Same place where the play *Hair* was booked. The emcee for one evening was Sugar Bear.

In 1969 the Doors arrived in Canada first and were escorted into Varsity Stadium. It was produced by Walker and Brower Productions. Kim Fowley was the emcee.

When John and Yoko and the band showed up, I got in the limo with John Brower along with Klaus Voorman and headed for the show. The Doors came in first and were met by the Vagabonds, a bike club in Toronto who gave them a 30-bike escort into Varsity Stadium.

We were driving and all along the way fans followed us. John told the driver of the limo to slow down because Yoko was six months pregnant. She was very friendly to me. John and I talked all about Gene Vincent and he said he couldn't wait to see him. He talked about times they used to play pool together 10 years ago in England.

In the car I played a tape of Elvis Presley singing the Beatles' "Yesterday" and "Hey Jude" from the 1969 show I saw Elvis do in Las Vegas at the International Hotel. I saw it weeks before and got a cassette of the show. John was amazed and could not believe it. He was really excited he was gonna see Gene Vincent. He wanted to be on the stage with Chuck Berry and Jerry Lee Lewis. So when we met up with Gene, he and Gene exchanged autographs. Eric Clapton was in another limo. We pulled in front of the stadium and a young girl yelled out, "It's John Lennon of the Beatles!" And all of a sudden there were bodies everywhere on top of the limo that we couldn't see out of it. We headed straight to the dressing room so that John could lie down for a while. We were greeted by Little Richard, Gene Vincent and Lord Sutch.

I stayed in a hotel and shared a room with Gene. I was in the room when Jerry Lee Lewis called Gene and I answered the telephone. "Hello. Is Gene there?" "Who is this?" "Just tell him it's 'The Killer' calling…"

Alice Cooper's band backed Gene and it was amazing. No rehearsals for anyone.

All the Doors and myself were onstage. I watched the Plastic Ono Band with Jim Morrison right at the side of the stage. And we really couldn't believe it. It sounded like music from the year 1992. Jim said after they left the stage, "You expect us to follow that?" Lots of people cheering.

It worked in a big stadium. Jim got a little snotty when Yoko started doing her whole thing. I don't think he was into that Bagism trip. Jim had cut his hair and shaved off his beard and looked really good. The Doors went on next and rocked that night. I had seen them in 1969 at the Aquarius Theatre in Hollywood and at Toronto they were pretty amazing

All the local papers in Los Angeles bad-rapped the show and said they were booed off the stage. Well, let me tell you it's a big lie because they weren't even attending. And I was.

Rob Hill, 2017, WHEN MORRISON MET LENNON

The Doors arrived at the Toronto International Airport mid-morning on September 13, where they were met by hundreds of bikers, a D.A. Pennebaker film crew, and two limos who were to escort the band to Varsity Stadium. What the band didn't know, though, was that this was a "dry run" for when John Lennon, Yoko Ono and the Plastic Ono Band, including Eric Clapton, who would be arriving later in the day. Promoter John Brower had pulled off a coup by calling Lennon at Apple Records a few days earlier asking if he wanted to emcee the gig; Lennon said no... but he would like to play! "We went from selling a couple thousand seats to selling 25,000 tickets when it was announced Lennon would play," said Brower.

While Morrison and the rest of the band watched the show by the edge of the stage through much of the day, Lennon was rushed into a makeshift VIP room: a spare smelly locker room full of socks, clothes and sports equipment. Morrison, just seven months from his Miami bust, had cut his hair a few days earlier; he took his shoulder-length hair into a ponytail himself and scissored it off, leaving him with an awkward and messy bob. He had also shaved his grizzly man beard he had been sporting for months, traded in his leathers for railroad striped trousers, and eschewed his snakeskin jacket for a shabby denim bomber. He looked more like a Northern California beatnik than an internationl rock 'n' roll star. As word finally made its way to a sullen Morrison that John Lennon was now going to play, he asked Bill Siddons to set up a meeting to discuss who would headline the show. Brower recounts:

"There was a knock on the locker room door and it was Bill [Siddons] and Morrison asking if they could talk to John and I. I grabbed John and we met in the hallway. The two singers didn't acknowledge each other or shake hands but

Siddons wanted to ask Lennon if the Doors could go on *before* Lennon. John's eyes opened wide and he said, 'No, *you* guys are the headliners, that means *you* go on last, that's the way it works.' John was not about to be upstaged by Morrison and whatever antics he might pull off. Just then, Little Richard appeared, and said to us, 'Hey, I will headline. I will headline.' I then told Morrison, 'Look, I have already paid you guys, so if you don't want to play, you can go back to your hotel room and relax, no problem.' Morrison nodded at Siddons and they agreed to go on after Lennon. Then Morrison said, 'One thing: We want to be on the side of the stage so we can watch the set.'

And, according to Kim Fowley, who was standing next to Morrison during the Plastic Ono Band's bizarre, impromptu set, the Lizard King said as Lennon was leaving the stage: "We have to follow *that!*"

Kim Fowley, 2009
in *MOJO* magazine

I was master of ceremonies in Toronto, Canada, at the Varsity Stadium. Bo Diddley, Junior Walker and the All Stars, Tony Joe White, Alice Cooper, Cat Mother and the All Night News Boys, Lord Sutch, Chicago Transit Authority, Chuck Berry, Jerry Lee Lewis, Gene Vincent—I was his record producer at the time—Little Richard, Doug Kershaw and the Doors.

I got the Toronto job because I was the voice of the Love-Ins in L.A. 1966, '67, '68 and '69. I did some pop festival shows with the Doors, the Seeds, Jimi Hendrix and the Jefferson Airplane. I did all those shows and knew what to do with a large audience like 100,000 people. Ritchie Yorke, *Billboard* editor in Canada, and a contributor to *Rolling Stone* and *NME* at the time, he knew about me and persuaded the promoters to hire me. $4,000 and a plane ticket. I also got a hotel room a week before the gig. My job was not only to announce the date but also be a consultant and tell them how things were going.

After Plastic Ono Band departed, I then said, "Get ready for the Doors, who are coming on next!"

The Doors started doing their thing. Around the third song of the set, out comes Chuck Berry, who saw the movie cameras, wanted to walk onstage, and approached Jim Morrison onstage and Jim Morrison stopped the show and said, "Chuck, you never let kids jam with you. You can't jam with us. Be nicer to kids and maybe someday we'll let you jam with us." And he was ordered off the stage by Jim Morrison. "Next time some guys want to jam with you, remember. Get off our stage." The place went wild.

They were the Doors. This was the year of the Miami Doors incident. So they did the Doors. This was going down in real time. It was music of the moment. It was the Arctic Monkeys playing. Current bands. Whoever was on the radio was suddenly in front of you. Or, what you remember from the radio years before in front of you. No passing of the baton or the end of the decade. Any of that. This is fun. Wow. I just saw a Beatle. I saw the Doors…

I remember a while afterwards, Ray Manzarek, who I knew from L.A., felt Lennon's appearance was some sort of psychic release from the pressures of being a Beatle.

In a non-paparazzi time of 1969, no one had the brains to photograph John Lennon and Jim Morrison together. Nobody has the picture, because no one thought of taking one, because there wasn't a paparazzi culture there to document it. They did speak because they had to, because one followed the other.

John Densmore Interview, 2009
in *MOJO* magazine

We came to Canada, and at the airport we all got into two black Cadillacs, then all of a sudden several hundred bikers started zooming along beside us, they were in a club called the Vagabonds. A hundred Hell's Angels types, and we're going, "Hey, this is kind of cool." And we come into the stadium, a football stadium, and they drive the limos all the way around the entire circle of the track with these 150 to 200 bikers leading us. So it's real profound. Like, "Oh my God. Here comes Lucifer," you know. It was really great.

So, I go backstage and Eric Clapton says to me, "Isn't this a crazy life?" I didn't get to see John. And we have to follow John and Yoko, and it's a monster band. Eric, Klaus, Alan. Ridiculous. They start and then we hear this noise coming out of the speakers. Everyone on the stage is saying, "What the fuck is going on here? Some feedback with their set?" And then everyone notices a bag on the floor of the stage with a wire leading from it. Yoko is in the bag with a microphone warbling. It was great. We didn't know what the fuck was going on. "Oh, wait a minute, she's in there." Really outrageous.

I mean, you know, John Lennon and the Plastic Ono Band walked out onstage and it was the biggest roar of the century, and we're supposed to follow this group?

Kim Fowley introduced us and we played the best we could. In my opinion we were fine. We weren't great. We weren't lousy. We were fine. But everyone was so in awe of the Mop Top... It was great.

D.A. Pennebaker Interview, 2012, in *Treats!* magazine

Q: Jim Morrison spoke to you about doing a documentary. In 1969 you saw the Doors in Toronto, where they shared the show with John Lennon and the Plastic Ono Band. But didn't film the Doors at this event.

A: Morrison had come to me a couple of times and he obviously was interested in doing a film. He and [Bob] Neuwirth came and showed me Jim's student film. I was not impressed, but that didn't mean anything. And I was interested in anybody who was a poet and wanted to make films. That was interesting to me. I didn't look down like this was amateur. But the fact is that he was a boozer. And, you know, that's a hard thing to make a film about. My father was a boozer. You can't count on getting their real lives. You get something else. They put on a kind of a show. And that was a problem.

And I had the same problem with Janis [Joplin]. The drugs. And I had nothing against drugs, because I didn't know enough about them yet. I loved Janis and thought she was a fantastic person. And I always thought there was a film there and I shot a lot with her, but what she was doing was so hard for her it was hard for me to film her.

And, Morrison was funded. He had some kind of money. And I had some concerns what he would look like in 20 years.

When the Doors got to Toronto, they were all very puffy. They looked like chefs in a big restaurant. And I would have shot them, but we couldn't afford to stay for the two days. But I heard them and we couldn't afford the tracking. We paid for the track for Yoko and John and gave it to them to release as a record.

John and Yoko performing in Toronto, it's an amazing thing. Coming at the end of that whole concert, it was the end of the Beatles. They understood it and at the end they fell silent. And John looked out and it was kind of scary and nobody was there. It was a funny moment. And they all left the stage, and I remember a piece of paper blowing across the stage and slowly the audience came to life. I thought, "My God. This is a fantastic wake." Yoko was so crazy, but still, there was something so fascinating about what she did. You could see she did it with absolute conviction. What she was bringing to me was a kind of funeral cry for something that was lost. At the time I wasn't sure how I felt about it. But I did welcome it.

Doors *Live in New York*, 2007
CaveHollywood.com

Rhino and Bright Midnight Archives have just issued the Doors' final tour with *Live in New York*. This six-disc collection contains all four of the Doors' performances—in their entirety—recorded in 1970 at the Felt Forum in New York City.

Recorded January 17 and 18, 1970—just a few weeks before the release of *Morrison Hotel*—these concerts find Jim Morrison, John Densmore, Robby Krieger and Ray Manzarek delivering smoking takes on soon-to-be-classics from their forthcoming album, including "Roadhouse Blues," "Peace Frog," "Ship of Fools" and "Maggie M'Gill."

The shows also implement a number of driving blues covers, such as Bo Diddley's "Who Do You Love," Howlin' Wolf's "Little Red Rooster" and John Lee Hooker's "Crawling King Snake." "Those were the bluesy songs we always used to do," Krieger says. "We probably hadn't done them in years, but we resurrected them for these shows."

The year prior to these shows, the Doors became one of the first rock bands to play New York City's Madison Square Garden. When they returned in 1970, Densmore says they chose to play the Felt Forum, a smaller venue than the Garden. "It was more intimate, and you could feel the audience more," he says. "There was more interaction, and the acoustics were much better, because it was designed for music."

Manzarek hails these shows as a return to the group's early days, when they used to play a small Los Angeles club called the London Fog. "I mean, talk about going back to basics. We used to do four sets a night at the London Fog, and we only had a small block of songs written up to that time. So we would do other people's material. And in New York, it was like the same thing. We've got four shows to play here, two sets tonight, two sets tomorrow night. Let's play whatever we want! Let's just go!"

And go they did. Along with a mix of then-unheard new songs and old covers, the band also tapped into its 1967, self-titled debut, peppering the set lists with signature songs such as "Break On Through (To the Other Side)," "Soul Kitchen," "The End," and "Light My Fire," the Doors' first No. 1 hit.

For the final show of the Felt Forum stand, the band was joined onstage by two guests: the Lovin' Spoonful's John Sebastian (who played harmonica on the studio version of "Roadhouse Blues") and drummer Dallas Taylor, who'd played on Crosby, Stills & Nash's debut. Sebastian sat in for "Rock Me" and was joined by Taylor for "Going to N.Y. Blues" and "Maggie M'Gill."

All four shows were mixed and mastered by the band's longtime engineer, Bruce Botnick, who recorded a number of shows from the Doors' 1970 tour on multi-track tape for the *Absolutely Live* album. While most of the music contained *on Live in New York* is unreleased, a few songs (and portions of songs) surfaced in 1970 on *Absolutely Live* and in 1997 on *The Doors Box Set.*

112

Sadly, these shows represent the Doors' final New York City performances with Morrison, who passed away July 3, 1971.

"Felt Forum," Ray Manzarek told me in a 2006 interview, "was, as Densmore said, 'our second annual appearance at Madison Square Garden.' We played there the January before and the January after. But we can't play in the basketball arena. That's for basketball players. Let's not play there unless we're gonna shoot hoops. And somebody said, "You know, they've got a Felt Forum, a 5,000-seat room. Perfect." And our manager said, "You're not going to get the same amount of money as you get in the big place. Unless you play four sets." Four sets? We'll do two a night.

And just run through all the blues 'cause we're going back to doing it the old way. "Let's play a lot of blues." It was really the Doors going back to their basic roots. Going back to blues and kick-arse rock 'n' roll. And we started off every set with a brand-new song no one had ever heard before, "Roadhouse Blues." It had not been released yet. It's a live concert and we owe that to Bruce Botnick. Who is still working with us to this very day. He's the guy who did the editing, the putting together and the sound mixing from *Live in New York*."

Felt Forum Ticket Stub
Courtesy of Ida Miller

111 C 11
SEC.   ROW   SEAT
ORCHESTRA $5.50
FELT FORUM
SUN. EVE.   18   10:00 P.M.
JAN.   1970
D | THE DOORS

Michael Simmons, 2006

I was almost 14 years old on Friday, January 24, 1969, when I saw the Doors perform at Madison Square Garden in New York City. Organist Ray Manzarek, guitarist Robby Krieger and drummer John Densmore were consummate musicians and the songs were perfect, but mostly I remember lead singer Jim Morrison standing stock-still in the center of the round stage. A fever drove me up out of my seat and I took off on a clean sprint toward The Doors.

Morrison had pipes that combined Sinatra and Howlin' Wolf, as well as a movie star mug—but there was more. Despite getting whacked in the belly with a cop's billy club for the crime of being young, I couldn't return to my seat. I staggered around until I was within a few feet of Jim. He was glowing—literally emitting heat—and I wasn't on drugs and it wasn't the dramatic light show.

Morrison sang lines from William Blake. I'd been reading Blake and Rimbaud and this young god before me embodied and projected the dead poets' ancient desire to transcend the ordinary and become divine. He was the single most charismatic human being I've ever seen and anything ordinary would remain my bête noire forevermore.

Dr. James Cushing, 2006

Why, this *Live in New York* at the Felt Forum box set is amazing. The group released six LPs in 1967–71, and this box contains six CDs recorded over two nights, so the first amazement lies in that proportion—it's as though the box were an act of magnification. The box presents all four shows in their complete running order, including Robby tuning up, crowd noises, moments when nothing at all seems to be happening. Then the band leaps into a song and the drama goes from zero to 9.9. Another amazement: the sudden switch from chaos to clarity.

(The programming function of the CD player is very helpful in this connection for overall listenability. One doesn't always want to sit through 2:23 of crowd noise before "Light My Fire," but the box shows such a respect for the historicity of the event as to constitute a third level of amazement.) The box proves that the Doors had a jazz flexibility in their set lists. No two shows are identical, and while songs are repeated, each traversal of them is interestingly different from each other and from the studio version.

I am reminded of the Miles Davis *Live at the Plugged Nickel* box set, which offers seven complete club sets from the 1965 MD Quintet recorded over two nights. (Miles actually repeated one set list song for song; the Doors didn't.) But jazz is supposed to use improvisation to deliver "the sound of surprise"; rock is supposed to dramatize the familiar in order to deliver The Hits You Love loud and live. The greatest amazement: how the Doors disregard that boundary, giving the Felt Forum audience, and now us, the jazz surprise and the hits in one dramatic moment.

Robby Krieger Interview on 1969's *Soft Parade* album
in *MOJO,* 2009

The Doors began recording *The Soft Parade* in November 1968 and completed it in July 1969.

The first single issued from the LP prior to *The Soft Parade* album release was "Touch Me," written by Robby Krieger. Another of his compositions, "Wishful Sinful," was a 45 RPM in February '69.

Q: Tell me about the pre-production process of *The Soft Parade* album.

A: When we started *The Soft Parade* it was after the Beatles' *Sgt. Pepper's*. *The Soft Parade* was recorded in West Hollywood at Elektra Sound Records on La Cienega Boulevard, produced by Paul Rothchild, who brought in arranger Paul Harris to do the string and horn overdubs.

I never liked the idea myself of strings and horns. It was an experiment. But once we decided to do it, we did it. In fact, we knew going in that the arrangements made for the songs were actually tailored to have strings and horns. I would work with Paul Harris 'cause I knew very little about orchestration. I would give him ideas for a horn line here and there and hope for the best. But he really did most of the work.

Q: Tell me about Paul Rothchild, who had produced albums by the Paul Butterfield Blues Band and Love.

A: Paul Rothchild was great. He was just what we needed. A very strong personality and real smart, which Jim looked up to. And he knew a lot about recording, you know, which we knew nothing about. There are very few guys that Jim would look up to, actually. And the same with us. He would make us do 50 takes. Bruce Botnick, our engineer for all the albums and the producer of *L.A. Woman*, is a little bit overlooked. He is a perfectionist. So is Paul. Bruce is the guy who actually turned the knobs, and you can't argue with the sound he got. He was very young but had produced the Supremes and a lot of stuff.

It was a blast to have Curtis Amy in the studio. That was the most fun part. You got to meet all these great musicians and hang out. They were our heroes. Like on "Touch Me," Curtis took the solo. That was the first time that happened. It served the song. That was another example of egos not getting in the way for the sake of the song. Leroy Vinnegar was on our *Waiting for the Sun* album. In fact, he played on "Spanish

Caravan," which was pretty silly 'cause it wasn't his type of forte.

The only reason we wanted a stand-up bassist was that it was right for the sound and Leroy was a good reader, and it was a written part. Probably any guy could have done it. Doug Lubahn and Harvey Brooks were the bass players on *The Soft Parade*. Leroy was a bit taken back when he saw what we wanted to do. "This isn't really my thing." "Come on, Leroy, you can do it." [Laughs.] Onstage we didn't have a bass player, just the three musicians. Ray covered it. There were a couple of other groups who did that, the Seeds and Lonnie Mack. I loved Lonnie. He played on "Roadhouse Blues."

Q: How was the material on *The Soft Parade* developed and constructed?

A: I came in with some songs, and it was not like I had not done that before, like "Love Me Two Times." It was more like coming up with stuff on my own. Jim was getting more and more hard to work with as far as songwriting goes. It wasn't the Jim who was writing "You're Lost Little Girl."

Q: Let's discuss the songs on the disc. "Tell All the People."

A: I had never written anything political and I heard this song by Leadbelly called "Fannin Street" about a street in New Orleans. And he had this line in there, "Follow me down." I really liked that line.

Q: Then the hit "'Touch Me."

A: It was originally called "Hit Me, Babe" and Jim thought people might take it literally on that. [Laughs.]

I remember seeing Otis at the Whisky. I was standing right in front of the stage for the whole show. I never heard of Otis Redding before and I was amazed at the energy that he created onstage. I would stand right there on the dance floor, stage right.

I wrote the song "Runnin' Blue" but when Jim [Morrison] started to sing it, he just came up with that Otis dead gone part right on the spot. Seemed to fit pretty good. So we left it in. I guess the horn parts reminded him of Otis.

Jim and I had a telepathic relationship. It was a perfect combo. That's how you make a great group. You have three, four or five guys who come together and have that perfect intuitive relationship and stuff comes out.

When we did the first Doors album Jim was totally unexperienced in the studio as far as recording his vocals. He had a year with his voice playing live every night. He had never done anything in the studio. And I think by the time *The Soft Parade* came around his voice had matured a lot as far as low notes and range. Stuff like that. I don't think he could have sung "Touch Me" nearly as good if that was on our first album.

Q: "Do It."

A: It started off with a lick that I had and we needed words for it. And I didn't have anything. And so we would go to Jim's poetry book. A lot of times that's what happened. Like with "Peace Frog."

That was different. It was a crazy little song that I had and when I sang it to the guys they really liked how I sang it. "You sound a little like Bob Dylan. Maybe you should sing that song." And then Jim added the part about Otis Redding. That's an example of how Jim would make my songs better. We had an ethic that we wanted to make the song better. Jim was amazing in that way. Possibly the least ego-bound

118

songwriter I have ever worked with, no question. As far as, "Hey… That's my line…" It wasn't like that at all. He was always open to discussion and for things I told him to sing. He wasn't really a musician, but usually what would happen is that he would come up with something better.

Q: "Wishful Sinful."

A: It's definitely one of my favorites on the album. The orchestration is really good. I love the chords and stuff I came up with on that song. I wish I knew how I did it. [Laughs.]

Q: "Wild Child."

A: It's one of my favorites because it's live. That one didn't need strings or horns. The title song "The Soft Parade" was quite a work. It was actually three songs in one.
          We didn't tour the *The Soft Parade* album. We only did it twice. It was another step for the Doors to try something different. The reason I didn't like it was that I felt we were kind of doing the album for somebody else. But I definitely like how it came out, you know. A couple of years later we tried remixing some stuff without the strings and horns, but it didn't quite work. We had actually tailored the arrangements to horns and strings, and to put that out again would be a lot of work, or alter the arrangements.

Tom Gundelfinger O'Neal Interview
Treats! magazine, 2012

          On December 4, 1968, I got into the *Smothers Brothers Comedy Hour* television show live taping on Beverly and Fairfax at Television City in Los Angeles. It was being aggressive. I bullshitted my way in. I found out the Doors were scheduled. You don't ask for the Smothers Brothers. You ask

119

to see the art director or the assistant director. When I wanted to do something for the Doors, I didn't go to Jim Morrison. I went to manager Bill Siddons. It's all about access.

I had seen the Doors perform at the Whisky a Go Go. I thought they had a hypnotic way. They made a big impression. And Jim seemed a little crazy. I was with a musician at the time watching the band, and the guy I was with was almost repulsed because Jim was starting to get in the vulgar side. So I saw this one side.

And then I had to figure out how to get real good access to these guys. And *The Smothers Brothers Comedy Hour* always had a rock act every week. How do I get in there? So I went to see the art director, maybe he would be interested in my photos. By then I was into psychedelia, since I was starting to take high-contrast photos and literally draw outlines in color on them. It was a mixture of psychedelics and graphics and I called them photographics.

The art director Romaine Johnson saw me and I then showed him some of them and he loved them. "Marty has to see these!" So Marty Pasetta, the director, and two guys, who were writers and helped produce the show. Marty was in a Nehru jacket. I made a presentation, with my beard and hair, and he loved my stuff. He flipped out on my stuff. He let me come up into the booth and watch rehearsal while he was calling camera angles. I loved the Smothers Brothers' show.

I had two meetings and got positioned. I showed them some of the Steppenwolf things I had done. I took high-contrast film. Koto litho film. I would take a negative in the enlarger and would make a positive off it. Now I make an inner negative. Any size. And getting very high contrast. Each generation the grays keep dropping out. Nobody in L.A. was doing anything like this. I was cleared to hang out and only shoot rehearsals. The show got ratings and freaks were allowed on the set.

Marty gave me permission. I'm there for the Doors' dress rehearsal. Jim arrived late. There's Jim sitting by himself. And I go over to sit down and started talking to him. He's totally different than the guy I had seen onstage. He's quiet, reserved and very nice. He never sat with the band. Five or six rows back of the band. They were clustered, kind of laughing.

The shot of Morrison looking over his left shoulder. There was a precise moment when he was doing that I caught it. It doesn't have a lot of animation but it has a moment. And that was a peak of a moment frozen in time.

And when it was time to do the live rehearsal, I got permission from Marty to take pictures while they did "Touch Me" with saxophonist Curtis Amy and the Smothers Brothers Orchestra.

Tommy Smothers was always running around. Steve Martin was there. David Steinberg. You couldn't hang out because it was very busy on the set.

I was shooting black and white. The color films were not suited for inside television photography. The five-grain color films did not have enough speed to shoot, so I was relegated to black and white.

CBS had their own staff photographer. I had to lay low. That photographer's union was so strong. I could have been expelled for my hair and clothes. I got that shit all the time.

Jim became a different person once the camera rolled. What really surprised me was for the on-air show, where he changed into a black shirt and cleaned up, he really got animated. They all got animated for the show, which was broadcast on December 15.

I would have liked to hang out with Manzarek, but it was hard for me then. I look back and I did some ballsy things. How am I gonna see the Doors? I'm going to go through the art director.

Jim Morrison, *Smothers Brothers Comedy Hour*, 1968
Photo by Tom Gundelfinger O'Neal

That was the last time I ever saw the Doors and Jim Morrison.

Seymour Cassell, 2014

I saw the Doors at the London Fog, the Whisky a Go Go. Jim had the same commitment to his art that Bob Dylan had. That any musician had. We would meet and read poetry on Sundays.

I could always get into the Whisky because Elmer Valentine and Mario at the door took care of me. We gave Elmer a piece of the Cassavetes film *Faces* so we could shoot at the Whisky. We also plastered posters of *Faces* on Sunset Boulevard.

I did a poetry reading with Jim, who was backed by Robby Krieger, at the Cinematheque 16 Theater, now on the property of Book Soup. It was a fundraiser for Norman Mailer's bid for mayor of New York City in 1969.

The guy who ran the Cinematheque 16 later had the Tiffany Theater, where *Faces* opened up, further up on Sunset. We had just met each other. It was a small town then. Jim was a big drinker. We all had become drinkers. He liked Jack Daniels. I know about the Love Street house. For this reading I did poems Jim gave me.

Michael C Ford, 2017

Here's the true story: Ray and I informally started a funk band in 1964 we named the White Trash Quintet (a name, incidentally, picked up and used by 1970s bands on more than one occasion) and we were playing at Mother Neptune's, a Beat Generation coffeehouse on Melrose Ave.

I saw the Doors, once at the London Fog and twice when they were the house band at the Whisky.

A few months later, returning this time from Weber College in Utah, looking up at a billboard on the Sunset Strip which stated THE DOORS BREAK ON THROUGH WITH AN ELECTRIFYING NEW ALBUM with four familiar faces emblazoned on the sign. And I do remember thinking, with the mote of a sentimental look in my eye, *Waitaminute, I know those guys.*

I remember being in an Elektra recording booth with Jim, during one of the *Waiting for the Sun* sessions. I was eyeballing this enlarged studio space with streamlined state-of-the-art sound equipment which looked (in retrospect) like something out of a *Star Wars* dashboard.

Mentioning this vastly enlarged version of earlier remembered Elektra studio surroundings, Morrison responded: "Yeah, 12 acid trips built this room!"

The very first time I read out loud in front of a live audience was a fundraiser for Norman Mailer's mayoral campaign in June of 1969 at the Cinematheque Theatre on Sunset Boulevard. And reciting my fledgling work alongside of Michael McClure, Jack Hirschman, three or four Andy Warhol experimental-film luminaries, Jim Morrison with Robby chording and single-string improvising on a Stratocaster. That was the night when Morrison recited the ENTIRE text of *American Prayer.*

Jack Larson, 2008

I was invited by Jim Morrison to Universal Studios to a projection room to see footage shot of their 1968 tour. Jimmy had invited me and Jim Bridges in '68 to see the Doors at the Hollywood Bowl. He got us great seats, but during "Light My Fire" the audience started throwing firecrackers and books of matches. I liked it but I knew by that time that he was unhappy with the whole scene.

The guy I saw in the projection room and at USC was totally different than the one in front of 18,000 people at the Bowl. By that time I knew him and realized why he was so disgruntled. He would talk about Rimbaud. He had a beard then, gained weight, and quiet.

Doors at the Hollywood Bowl July 5 1968
Photo by Henry Diltz

In February 1969 I saw the Living Theater on the campus of USC at Bovard Auditorium with Jimmy. Le Living. We went together. They all exposed themselves. I found Jimmy to be very genuine and I liked him very much.

I had a play at the Mark Taper Forum. A group of one-acts with playwright Harvey Perr. He wrote for the *Los Angeles Free Press* and he knew Jimmy Morrison. And Harvey had this play and we were on the same bill at the Mark Taper and Morrison came down with Harvey and I got to know him. He was enormously friendly to me.

The irony about Jimmy Morrison is that I'm part of an award that is given out, the James Bridges award, that is given out to a filmmaker, and I go to this awards ceremony and about five years ago there is a James and Pamela Morrison award. I then ask the development woman, "What is this? I knew Jim went to UCLA and the film school." Pam's family have established a film award for 5 or 10 thousand dollars, or something, UCLA, James and Pamela Morrison.

Randall Jahnson Interview, 2017

(screenwriter for the 1991 movie, *The Doors*)

Q: You attended the UCLA film school. We keep reading about NYU Film School. But UCLA Film School made impact.

A: Francis Ford Coppola, Colin Higgins, Penelope Spheeris, Paul Schrader, Gore Verbinski, Alex Cox, Charles Burnett, Tim Robbins, Alison Anders, Shane Black, Rob Reiner, David Koepp, Alexander Payne... the list of UCLA grads goes on and on.

And there are many, many alumni who are not household names but have extremely successful careers in all areas of the industry—agents, writers, production managers and designers, sound recordists and mixers, cinematographers, editors, special effects...

Q: You had two teachers Ray and Jim had. Can you offer things that you learned from the two instructors that informed your career and might have educated Ray and Jim earlier?

A: The two instructors were Ed Brokaw and Lou Stoumen. Both were still teaching at the film school when I attended from 1979 to '82.

I think I took "Introduction to Screenwriting" from Stoumen. He was an Academy Award–winning documentary filmmaker, writer, and photographer—hard to categorize because he had done so many things in different disciplines.

He'd been a combat correspondent-photographer for *Yank* magazine in World War II; wrote, directed, and produced about 90 short films. Physically, he was striking—tall, thick black hair with a gray beard, face etched with lines—very much how I'd imagined Captain Ahab (sans the peg leg). Yet he was soft-spoken, humble. A gentle soul with a definite counterculture streak. I remember meeting with him in his book-cluttered office once. I noticed one of his Oscars resting on the windowsill. It had a string of beads around its neck.

Stoumen published a book in 1988 titled *Journey to Land's End*. It's a poetic, loose narrative illustrated with 90 of his black-and-white photos (Ed Brokaw and Lou's office are the subjects of two of them). He subtitled it "a paper movie." On the back cover are endorsements from Laura Huxley, Ray Bradbury and Ansel Adams—not a bad fan club.

Recently, when I cracked it open and read some of its passages for the first time in years, I was reminded of Morrison's *The Lords and the New Creatures*—not so much for its similarities in cadence and observational musings, but its aesthetic, its vibe. Of course, Stoumen's book came out many years after Morrison's—and one could argue who influenced whom—but I suspect that Stoumen's post-Beatnik, early-'60s sensibility made an impact—however large or small—on that pudgy kid from Florida.

If the film school had a keystone, it was Ed Brokaw. I doubt there's anyone who went through the program who'd disagree. Taking his editing class and cutting on the Moviola an action sequence from *Gunsmoke* were a rite of passage. He possessed an encyclopedic knowledge of all aspects of filmmaking. From what I understand, it was Brokaw who really conceived of and shaped the school's curriculum so that everyone who graduated would be a complete filmmaker.

Like Stoumen, he was a World War II veteran. He had served in the Army Signal Corps in Burma. After the war he attended the UCLA film school and graduated in 1952, then joined the faculty. He taught there a couple years then moved to New York and ran his own production company. In 1961 he rejoined the UCLA faculty and stayed until his retirement in 1988.

He was avuncular in appearance. Balding, rosy-cheeked. Always in a collared shirt and tie. Corduroy coat. I used to see him walking the streets of Westwood at all hours of the day and night. Sometimes he'd be quietly talking to himself. There were rumors he lived out of his office. Indeed, a strategically placed Oriental folding screen blocked the view to the interior whenever he emerged. I remember passing it once in the dead of night while taking a break from editing and hearing a blistering jazz (*Impressions*-era Coltrane, maybe) coming from behind the door.

His lectures could be meandering esoteric excursions incorporating the work of John Cassavetes, his wartime experiences, close encounters with John Coltrane and Miles Davis (he was a big jazz fan), and the grain count of a specific film stock.

Brokaw had the reputation of having been Morrison's favorite instructor—at least according to Jerry Hopkins and Danny Sugerman in *No One Here Gets Out Alive.* That may or may not have been true—but I do know that when I met Ray Manzarek for the first time, we talked about Brokaw and Ray spoke of him in an almost reverential tone. The fact that we'd both taken his classes—albeit a good 15 years apart— immediately established a bit of a rapport; it might have even helped me land the job of writing the script.

When I interviewed him in 1986, Brokaw was 69 years old and professor emeritus. I met him at the North Campus area of UCLA. We spoke for about an hour. He described Manzarek as very cinematic in his thinking, a natural filmmaker. Morrison, however, was not. His ideas were too abstract, too complex to translate onto the screen. That's why poetry was a much better form of expression for him.

Brokaw led me to a nearby patch of grass and proceeded to walk off the exact dimensions of Bungalow 3K7, the Quonset hut that had once stood there, housing the film school at the time Morrison and Manzarek had attended. Next he vividly described its interior. He finished by pointing out where the port-a-potty that serviced the department had been erected.

On the inside of its door, he recalled gleefully, was a graffiti that read, "Jim Morrison has the ass of an angel." He said after Bungalow 3K7 was torn down, the door to that crapper mysteriously appeared in the lobby of the film school's new building, Melnitz Hall. It lasted there for a while—perhaps as a waggish tribute to the school's famous alumnus—before it disappeared forever.

Ray had Renoir as a teacher. And Josef Sternberg was also there.

Both were long gone before I got there—but that exemplifies the UCLA program, bringing in legendary filmmakers to educate the next generation. The goal, I think, was to create "auteurs."

Q: Do you have a theory why various DVD and video products on and by the Doors translated so well?

A: They were a band that transcended rock music and entered mainstream culture. This was due in part, of course, to Morrison's good looks and premature exit, but also to the timelessness and theatricality of their music and to their intersection and experimentation with film.

With Manzarek and Morrison being film school graduates, they had an awareness and an understanding of the power of cinema and visual media. Plus, they were very well documented. Their close friends from film school, Frank Lisciandro and Paul Ferrara, along with Babe Hill, shot a ton of performance and behind-the-scenes footage of them, which culminated in the experimental documentary *Feast of Friends*.

Later on they collaborated on *HWY*, their attempt—and arguable failure—at a narrative film. Morrison sunk his own money into that, I think, which shows how committed he was. Lisciandro also captured a wealth of images with his still-shot camera. To this day he continues to unveil new photos he took back then. Most have been compiled in several excellent books.

While Morrison's student film has famously gone MIA, Manzarek's two 16mm efforts, *Evergreen* and *Induction*—both excellent—were carefully kept and have been included as extras on some documentary and concert compilations.

So heading into the 1980s and '90s they had a ton of visual material available for issue on VHS and later on DVD. Much of it was cut into individual videos for airplay on MTV, which also helped to introduce the band to a whole new generation.

Add to that "The End" opening *Apocalypse Now* in 1979 and their legacy was further cemented in popular culture.

Two things come to mind as I think about this. I remember Lou Stoumen discussing *Apocalypse Now* in class right after its release (he'd also had Coppola as a student). He felt it was a flawed film. On the whole, it couldn't measure up to the brilliance of its beginning.

Secondly, I recall Manzarek telling me that he read an early version of *Apocalypse Now* by John Milius that used "Light My Fire" in the opening sequence instead of "The End." It described Willard and his squad rising out of a rice paddy to ambush a unit of North Vietnamese. They return to base, hoisting the scalps of their enemies. Willard yells, "Hit it!" and "Light My Fire" begins to play over the base loudspeakers as a kind of victory celebration. Vintage Milius. Ray thought it was very intense, but liked it.

Q: Do you have a theory why the Doors' library continues to sell and reach new ears?

A: Well, it certainly helps to have your charismatic frontman die young. And to have your music bookend an iconic movie—not to mention all the books.

But really I attribute their continued popularity to one primary source: Ray Manzerek. Ray was the Keeper of the Faith. Long after Jim dropped off the planet, and Robby Krieger and John Densmore segued into other interests, Ray kept the fires burning.

Anyone who listened to FM radio in the late '70s, '80s and '90s inevitably encountered his rich baritone on classic rock stations waxing poetic about Jim, Dionysus, and the road to excess leading to the palace of wisdom. And with a storyteller's gravitas, he would often conclude these interviews by titillating our imaginations with the possibility that Jim might not even be dead but living in self-exile in some exotic location like the Seychelles.

It didn't hurt that he was producing X and the Jim Carroll Band, either. X covered "Soul Kitchen" on their iconic first album, further extending the Doors' reach and street cred.

In a sense, Ray—with the later assistance of Danny Sugerman—made the Doors a brand, and protected and marketed them as such. I always like to point out that before film school, Ray received a degree in economics from DePaul University. He knew the value of a dollar.

Don't get me wrong—I really liked and respected Ray. I'd go over to his place in Beverly Hills and we'd talk about all sorts of stuff from basketball to movies and punk rock—great conversations. But when it came to Morrison and the Doors, he was a bit of a broken record (pun intended). To really go deep, I realized early in my research, I would have to seek out other sources.

Q: Walk me through the process of writing the movie. Early draft(s) and concepts suggested, and then the next step with Oliver Stone.

A: I was hired to write the screenplay in early 1986. One of the things I was most excited about was the opportunity to create a rock 'n' roll epic. Something with scope. I felt that hadn't really been done before.

I also wanted to bring a real visceral and surreal—if not full-on hallucinatory—quality to the movie. It had to be a trip. I wanted to convey the passion of a live show. To smell the smoke and the sweat, and I especially wanted the music to sound live with all its imperfections—nothing canned.

At that time I had just finished making music videos for Henry Rollins and Black Flag and the Minutemen. The L.A. punk scene had made a big impression on me, and I wanted to bring that energy to the script. In fact, when I met Ray, Robby, and John Densmore for the first time I told them I thought the Doors were far more punk and beatnik than they were hippie and flower power. I even went out on a limb and said someone like Rollins should play Morrison—not an established movie star. They agreed. (Some time later I took Rollins with me to meet Ray and Paul Rothchild at a recording studio. He was stoked!)

Anyway, once my deal was signed, lead producer Sasha Harari told me, "Take a couple weeks to research, then go write the script." Back then there was no internet, and there were no biographical materials available on Morrison save for a few magazine articles and the Hopkins/Sugerman book, which we didn't have the rights to. So that meant I had to do my own footwork.

After some initial interviews with the surviving Doors, both collectively and individually, and with Paul Rothchild, I had a very strong sense that this story was much deeper than anyone realized. So instead of taking a couple of weeks, I took several months to research, ultimately compiling about 50 hours of taped interviews. I met Jim's parents. Pamela's parents. Bill Siddons. Babe Hill. Jac Holzman. Jim's lawyer at the Miami trial, Max Fink. And many more. Some were very enlightening, others were not.

This process would have continued had it not been for Harari and Columbia Studios development exec Jude Schneider imploring me, "Enough with the damn research— start writing the script!"

The issue was simple: Despite all these interviews, a clear portrait of Morrison was still not emerging. I was reminded of the old anecdote about the blind men touching the elephant. Each one held a different part of its body—the tail, the trunk, a tusk, an ear—and each one announced that he knew the true nature of the beast. Of course, all of them were wrong. No one had a clue what it really was.

There were other challenges too, chief of which was how to structure the screenplay. Where should it start? (I hated cradle-to-the-grave biopics.) How should it depict his premature death? If the movie proceeded linearly, then you run the risk of ending on a major bummer. How do you put a positive spin on a guy who was dead in a Paris bathtub at 27?

The answers started coming when I got the transcript for the session in which Jim recorded all his poetry—the stuff that eventually landed on the posthumous *An American Prayer* album. I was really moved by the fact that here was this guy, at the height of his fame and fortune, choosing to spend what would be his last birthday alone in a dark studio with an engineer recording his poetry. I got the feeling that he knew he wouldn't be around for much longer; he was putting down his last will and testament, and he wanted this to be his legacy.

He recorded a ton of material in that session, most of which has since been published. There's a photo of him taken by Lisciandro, I think, at a nearby Mexican restaurant, the

Lucky U. He's sitting with a plate of enchiladas and a beer smiling into the lens—and he just looks really happy. Suddenly, I had the framing device for the movie. It would start with him coming into the studio and end with him, satisfied that his legacy was secure, leaving to get a taco. And we would revisit the session throughout the movie so the poetry itself—Jim's own words—would provide a kind of running commentary to the narrative.

My producer didn't like it. His chief complaint was how Morrison looked at the time. He was bearded, overweight, haggard. He said people didn't want to see that at the start of the movie; they wanted to see the hot, sexy, leather-clad rock god. "But that's the drama," I argued. "How did he go from the Lizard King to this tragic broken figure?" Harari couldn't be persuaded. As I divulged more of my research, which further contradicted the public perception of Morrison, he warned me that if I persisted with this approach I would be fired. I persisted. And after delivering my drafts I was promptly fired.

They threw out my script and hired and fired two other writers who wrote their own drafts. Then three and a half years later, I was at Cafe Largo, a club on Fairfax Avenue, seeing poet and Morrison friend Michael C Ford perform. I had interviewed Ford as part of my research and we had become friends. That night Ray Manzarek accompanied him on piano. During a break, Ray saw me and pulled me aside. "You're gonna get a call from Oliver Stone," he said. I was aware that Stone had come aboard on the project.

Ray said Stone had asked to read all the previous scripts by all the previous writers, and then in a recent pre-production meeting announced he liked mine the best and was going to work off it. Sure, Ray, I thought. Why would the hottest filmmaker in town need to talk to me? Well, Ray was right. About a week later I got a call from Stone's office and a meeting was set.

I met Stone at his production company office in Santa Monica. He was curious about a lot of my research, especially Jim's antics in the bedroom. I told him I had my sources. He asked me who they were. I replied I couldn't reveal their names—the women had spoken to me in confidence. Suddenly the meeting was over. Rising from his desk, he finished by saying that he was going to write his own draft of the script, but "yours has inspired me a great deal, and when it's all said and done, I think the Writers Guild will be very good to you." (The Guild determines screenplay credits on films where there have been multiple writers.)

I left. I'd been there less than a half-hour.

Q: Do you have a Val Kilmer story or anecdote?

A: I don't. I never had the opportunity to meet him. But I was certainly impressed by his performance—both his acting and his singing.

Q: Were you invited to the set for filming? Do you have an anecdote?

A: No, I was never on the set. At the time cameras were rolling, per Writers Guild protocol, final screenplay credits had yet to be determined so I was kind of a non-entity. A good friend of mine from film school was on the set, though, serving as camera assistant for DP Robert Richardson. He kept me apprised when he could.

Q: The focus of media and legacy is often on Jim. We know it was a team effort.

A: Absolutely. It's hard to imagine the band without one of its members—each played an essential role, each brought a unique point of view. The Doors themselves recognized that;

135

that's why there are no individual songwriting credits (apart from the covers of "Back Door Man" and "Alabama Song") on the first three albums. All titles were attributed to "The Doors."

Nevertheless, it is interesting to note that of the band's many hits Robby wrote the three biggest—"Light My Fire," "Touch Me" and "Love Her Madly"—demonstrating that it wasn't all the Jimbo show. (On Morrison's insistence, the band changed to individual writing credits for *The Soft Parade*; Morrison didn't like "Touch Me" and didn't want to be perceived as its writer.)

Speaking of Robby, producer Paul Rothchild told me in an interview that in many ways he felt Robby was the "real Door." Jim got all the press, but it was Robby who exemplified what the band espoused. He was the true psychedelic adventurer and sexual experimenter. You just never heard about it because by nature Robby was very shy, retiring.

And of course no discussion of the Doors can ever be complete without acknowledging the enormous contribution of the production team of Rothchild and engineer Bruce Botnick. In the minds of many, they were the fifth and sixth members of the band. I met Botnick briefly once, but never had the opportunity to sit down with him. I interviewed Rothchild at length on several occasions. He was very insightful, a great storyteller. In fact, he said he'd recently stopped smoking pot, which he dearly loved, because it was affecting what he loved most of all—his ability to converse.

On the topic of the first album he described a moment that I feel sheds light on his/their whole approach to recording music. When they first got into the studio, he said Robby was eager to use a wah-wah pedal, which was very popular then. Rothchild immediately put the kibosh on that and announced to everyone that they were not going to indulge in any trendy tricks or toys; their aim was a classic sound, a record and music that would stand the test of time. He wasn't against innovation; he was against the ear candy that can cheapen and distract from the underlying substantive material. That's something I've never forgotten. And in this age of pervasive media and dazzling effects and easy apps, it really bears keeping in mind.

Q: Can you offer anything about the myth and media creation of Jim as opposed to the guy you sort of learned about during research and meeting family and band members?

A: That dichotomy was the central conflict in my drafts of the script.

Morrison couldn't ultimately live up to the mythic figure of himself that the media and fans expected and perpetuated. Once he spawned the Lizard King, there was no putting that genie back in the bottle. At first it was fun, exhilarating. My sense is that he saw himself as a kind of deliverer; he was going to take his audience somewhere they had never gone before, and together they would return enlightened. But his creation grew into something he had no control over and became untenable.

Out of all the conflicting interviews I compiled about Morrison, two characteristics consistently emerged: One, he was very, very bright; again and again, I heard statements like "He was the smartest guy I ever met" and "I never saw him without a book in his hand"; two, he was honest, honest to the point of being brutal. And he would not suffer fools.

I suspect at some point he knew he was living a lie—he was no Lizard King, he could not deliver what he'd promised—and that weighed heavily on him. Being as brutally honest as he was, I imagine he was most brutal on himself. And that's where the drinking and the self-destructive behavior came in.

The movie covered this to a point where I felt it was overdone, especially his downward spiral. Granted, Morrison drank—but if Oliver had just substituted a book for a fifth of booze in a few scenes we might have come away with a better portrait of him. Also, I don't buy that Jim was as death-obsessed as the movie made him out to be. (The pervasive bald-headed death figure was Oliver's addition.) In fact, I feel the real Morrison was just the opposite—he found life mysterious and amazing and was drawn to characters like Ed Brokaw or Lou Stoumen or Max Fink and poet Michael McClure because they seemed to have mastered it in some way.

One of my favorite images of him is in *Feast of Friends*. He's got a paperback in his hand and he's talking (backstage?) to a priest who's smoking a pipe. They seem to be engaged in a deep discussion. Listening, Jim shifts and cocks his head like he's having his mind blown, then he seems to be passionately articulating something. That to me is the essence of the guy. A seeker with an unquenchable thirst for knowledge, pure experience.

I'll wrap this up with something his mother, Clara, told me. I was interviewing her and his father, Steve Morrison, in the office of their attorney in Century City. A condition of their deal was that they would not be depicted in the film except for the famous—or infamous—Indians-on-the-highway scene. So when I asked about it, they gave their recollection. It was fuzzy, at best.

Clara, who did most of the talking, described them driving in New Mexico or Arizona. Steve was at the wheel, she was in the passenger seat. Jim, around 4 years old then, was in the backseat with his grandparents. They vaguely recalled having to slow down because an old pickup truck was parked on the side of the road with a group of Native Americans standing around it. There was no accident, though, no carnage, no "Indians scattered on dawn's highway bleeding." But there was something eerie in the air, she added. The Indians were keening. And perhaps that strange wailing made an impact on her impressionable young son.

Then she looked at me and said, "Little Jimmy had a tendency to embellish."

Out of all the interviews I did, I think that's my favorite comment about him. It just cracks me up. I think it's spot-on and reminds us that Morrison, at his core, was a storyteller. As with Huck Finn, there was a streak of the unreliable narrator in him. A prankishness. He could pull your leg. And what is a storyteller anyway, but a philosopher and an artist and a teacher in the guise of an entertainer?

That's how I like to see Jim Morrison.

Jim Morrison at Thee Experience by **Kirk Silsbee,** 2017

After the Doors had tasted success, Hollywood was Jim Morrison's playground. The Whisky a Go Go in West Hollywood, which launched the band, showcased all the important groups with label backing. After the Doors had outgrown clubs, Morrison had carte blanche at the Whisky; his star cache was his gold card. Occasionally he'd perform, but most of the time he just got drunk and abused the people around him.

In 1969, he was one of the notables who might be glimpsed at Thee Experience, the last psychedelic rock club in Hollywood. Situated farther east than the fabled Sunset Strip, at the shabby corner of Sunset Boulevard at Sierra Bonita Avenue, its brief life fit neatly within the year 1969. From March to December the club booked second-drawer bands, though some were memorable: Flying Burrito Brothers, Alice Cooper, Poco, Buddy Miles Express, Blues Image, T. Rex, and the Bonzo Dog Band. Blues stars John Lee Hooker, Bo Diddley, Albert Collins, Big Mama Thornton and Slim Harpo also played there.

But the bands were almost superfluous. What drew people to Thee Experience were the superstars who came to jam and party. Led Zeppelin, Jimi Hendrix, Jagger and

Richards, Janis Joplin, Spencer Davis, Carlos Santana, Frank Zappa, Jorma and Jack of the Jefferson Airplane, Jerry Garcia, Captain Beefheart, and Booker T were just some of the rock royalty who dropped in. English musicians, in particular, loved the place: English breakfasts were served to them in the wee hours when the audiences had gone home.

Marshall Brevetz was the heart and soul of Thee Experience. The 29-year old ex-Marine had been Miami's biggest rock impresario, where he helmed Thee Club and the Miami Pop Festival. Looking like a pot-bellied Larry of the Three Stooges, Brevetz kept the club alive through wheeling and dealing. He catered to the whims of his star clientele, hoping that it would eventually boost his bottom line. It never did.

Habitually clad in Bermuda shorts, Brevetz was also a soft touch for the many runaways who gravitated to Thee Experience. They were on the run from the law, from the draft, from their families—lost millionaires and lost indigents.

His wife Marsha ran the kitchen, concocting delicacies—banana splits and hamburgers. A classic earth mother, she would console a drunken Morrison when he'd wallow in the melancholy of familial strife back in Florida. At the Whisky, he had to be stoned or drunk to perform. At Thee Experience, he grooved on Marsha's nurture and French toast.

Though Morrison occasionally sat in at Thee Experience—like with future War harmonica ace Lee Oskar and Blues Image drummer Joe Lala—he usually went there to carouse. To his credit, Morrison always paid his bill at the club—unlike most of the gold-plated guests.

One of the people who visited the club's kitchen was Owsley Stanley. The little man who dosed the whole West Coast with purple LSD traveled with the Grateful Dead. At Thee Experience, he liked to inhale the gas from whipped cream cans. Leaning against the refrigerator door, he mischievously spooned ice cream into the mouths of anyone he could surprise. Peggy, a waitress, thought it was cute that he plied her with ice cream bites with each trip to the kitchen. It wasn't long before she found herself transfixed by the pretty colors of a hamburger, then slowly becoming terrified that the burger was trying to kill her.

The large room was darkened but the waitstaff passed by the bleacher section, a virtual black hole, to reach the kitchen. It was something of a gauntlet, as they were sometimes pawed, abused, or exposed to sexual acts and inebriated behavior.

Those bleachers saw some after-hours action too. The big-hearted Brevetz might provide crash space to a dishwasher under the bleachers. After-hour trysts, consummated on and under them, were also common.

But wild scenes were *de rigueur* at Thee Experience. Drummers John Bonham and Keith Moon acted like drunken lunatics, and drugs were plentiful. A tall, slender groupie named Dani spent a lot of time under a table occupied by a superstar English band... before they had her on a table top. Bluesmen John Lee Hooker and Earl Hooker had simultaneous fun with a smiling GTO in the storeroom behind the bar. A Canadian band argued and physically fought over drugs.

Women dropped like flies at the sight of Jim Morrison. Peggy the waitress had seen the Doors at the Cheetah in 1967, and had loved him from afar. She finally met him at a Bel Air party about the time the club opened, and discovered they shared Florida roots. Even drunk, she thought he was the most beautiful man she'd ever seen. A few nights later, at another party, they had a quiet, intimate talk. Their time together lasted about a week. It wasn't long before he appeared at Thee Experience with other women and paraded them before her. After a tearful Peggy pulled her apron and went home crying, Ellyn the ticket-taker—in a show of sisterhood—got him alone and really told him off. Like a naughty boy chastised, he contritely listened.

He didn't charm them all. Waitress Jaki Read said in 2009: "I didn't care for Jim Morrison. He was like those really smart-ass high school boys who could quote Shakespeare but didn't really understand what they were talking about. When you questioned them about it, you found that they really didn't understand the work to any degree of depth. They were empty but rapid talkers; that was Jim Morrison. If we ever spoke at length, I was usually testing him. He tried to make fun of my boyfriend, Joe Lala, once. Now, Joe was 20 years old and had no intellectual pretensions of being anything other than what he was: a musician. Morrison made some sly comment about Joe being a lightweight and I threw him out of the house."

London transplant Sally Stevens didn't know who the Lizard King was when she took a waitress job at Thee Experience that summer. Brevetz showed her his photo, and told her to be on the lookout for him.

One night, as a favor, Stevens filled in for a waitress whose little boy was sick. Delaney & Bonnie and Friends were the marquee attractions that Memorial Day weekend; drop-ins included Hendrix, Zappa, Steve Stills and Dave Mason. Stevens navigated past the bleachers with extra caution. A loud group of drinkers were becoming out of control. One bearded drunk kept moving his chair further into the aisle, complicating her movement. When her path was blocked entirely, she turned to retreat down the aisle. Her hair was grabbled from the back and Stevens was pulled violently down backwards onto the bearded bear's lap, where he yelled, "Get me a beer, bitch!!" The quick-thinking woman jumped up and kicked the chair over, with her drunken assailant in it. Then she hit him in the nose with her tray for good measure.

Shocked, but also furious, she stormed into the kitchen and slammed down her tray. Sally was livid and could take no more that night. The next day she was informed that she was fired. She also learned for the first time that her shrouded antagonist was Jim Morrison.

Robert Hawkins was the doorman that night, and said of Jim in 2009. "He did that more than once," adding, "and he only did it with girls. No one was shocked, no matter what he did. We were called to take care of unruly people but not a Jim Morrison. He and all the other stars that came in had free rein; they did whatever they wanted. It didn't matter to Marshall. He kowtowed to all the stars."

Stevens had come to Hollywood to find work in the music industry, but after her firing, she found it hard to get a job. She also thought that Morrison had a hand in her difficulties. After six months, she ran into Doors producer Paul Rothschild at the Troubadour. He offered her a job at Elektra Records, assisting office manager Susan Helms.

One day at the switchboard, the "night line" connected to the studios lit up. When Sally answered, "Good afternoon, Elektra Records…" a voice on the other end asked for her. When it identified itself as Jim Morrison, she thought it was a prank and promptly hung up. But the line rang back with the same plea: *Jim Morrison to speak with Sally Stevens.* When she asked for some personal information to verify, he said softly: "I got you fired at Thee Experience." Soft-spoken and sober, Jim said he'd been trying to find her for six months to apologize.

Stevens read him the riot act, and Morrison took his medicine. But he was in a thoughtful mode, and they wound up spending an hour on the phone together. He checked in with her every few weeks to chat and they developed a casual phone relationship—Morrison knew he could get a straight answer from Sally if he was unsure about an aspect of his life and career. She recognized his intellect—head and shoulders over the average rocker's—and told him that he was getting a little old for some of the rock-star shenanigans he'd been dabbling in. Morrison agreed it was time for a change, and the subject of Paris came up.

Kurt Ingham, 2015

On July 5, 1971, when the Telex communiqué came to the Elektra office, reporting Jim Morrison's death, Jaki Read was the first to see it.

Kurt Ingham, 2015

I met Jim Morrison 1970 when I was taking pictures in conjunction with a Salli Stevenson interview for *Circus* magazine. We got along quite well—both similar in age, former UCLA film students, generally artsy types.

The Doors office on Santa Monica Boulevard was pretty close to where I lived in Laurel Canyon, so it was easy to drop by to watch rehearsals or look at proof sheets.

At one point after a short rehearsal and perusal, Jim suggested we adjourn to the Phone Booth, a topless bar conveniently across the street. I don't recall who went with us, but I don't think it was members of the band.

Jim was quite popular with the waitresses, and it was an amusing contrast to see one table filled with laughing boisterous longhairs while the others were occupied by slightly furtive besuited businessmen.

At that time I was more a smoker than a drinker, and we got pretty silly, pretty fast. Jim was planning to go to Italy. Since I had lived in Rome for a few months, he insisted I give him travel tips.

This evolved into an Italian language lesson, which consisted of us shouting any Italian word we could think of, with an an exaggerated accent: "Pizza! Lambretta! Spaghetti! Ferrari! Macaroni!," etc. We both found this quite hilarious!

When I left the darkened club I was in for a shock! Outside was still daylight—and I had never before been inebriated when the sun was out! I crawled into my 1965 Mustang Fastback and managed to get home sans incident.

Jim Morrison photo courtesy of Kurt Ingham

Anne Moore Interview, 2017

I first met and knew Anne Moore as a music journalist in late 1969 and was aware that she kept a diary and collected pop culture artifacts, even keeping press releases and envelopes from record companies.

I have a vivid recollection from 1970 of walking on Hollywood Blvd. and bumping into Rodney Bingenheimer on his way to Lewin Record Paradise. We were both going to check out English import albums. Rodney was writing for *GO!* magazine. He enthusiastically proclaimed "I just saw the writer Anne Moore with Jim at Duke's Coffee Shop on Santa Monica Blvd." It took me 48 years to figure out Rodney was referring to Jim Morrison!

Envelope courtesy of Anne Moore

Q: Anne, you had been writing for music periodicals in the mid-'60s. Right?

A: My first byline was with my friend, Jennifer Starkey, for an article in the October 1965 issue of *Teen Screen*. I wrote dozens of articles and columns for *Teen Screen* and *IN* (fashion/teen girls/same publisher) and eventually became editor for both publications. I wrote for *World Countdown*, *FAVE* (staff/sister magazine to *Tiger Beat*), *Phonograph Record Magazine*, *Creem*, *L.A. Image*, *Fusion*, *Date Book* and many more. I didn't

146

start out to be a music journalist, but I had always wanted to be a writer. I sort of fell into all of this because of my love of music and the whole cultural scene. Or you can just blame it on the Beatles and several lucky circumstances.

In early 1971 I started working for United Artist/ Liberty/Blue Note Records as their National Director of College Promotion. I ran that department and traveled all over the United States for the company for several years.

Q: Did you see the Doors at Ciro's, the London Fog or Whisky a Go Go in 1966? If so, what did you think of them? And how did you meet Jim?

A: The first time I saw the Doors perform was at the Whisky sometime early in the summer of '66. The Buffalo Springfield were headlining that week and my friend, writer Jennifer Starkey, who worked for their management company, Greene and Stone, invited me down to the club to see them. She knew I'd enjoy the Springfield and promised I'd really like the other group playing with them too, the Doors.

The Doors were different. They were a combination of diverse influences that made their sound unique. That sounds like a music critic's cliché review, an overall generic description, but it's true and many critics did describe them that way. The Doors didn't sound like any other band out there, not even when they did a traditional blues number. There was little to no talk onstage the night I saw them, and I don't even remember them announcing the song titles. Very laid back, no craziness that night, just good music, that's where the energy came from. The audience loved them. My friend was right, I really liked the Doors. And the Buffalo Springfield were pretty good too.

I was busy with college, writing and traveling during the next couple of years, so I never saw the wild Jim Morrison/ Lizard King persona live—with those crazy stage antics fueled by drugs and booze. I missed that whole wild Dionysian era, thank goodness. Meanwhile, the Doors were all over the radio, top of the charts, darlings of the rock scene. I saw them on TV, heard the wild stories, but missed the crazies.

Q: And you caught the 1968 Doors.

Ticket courtesy of Ida Miller

A: The second time I saw the Doors perform live was later at the Inglewood Forum in L.A. near the end of '68. I went to the show with a couple of friends, and I had an extra ticket so I asked Michael Bruce, who played keyboards/guitar for Alice Cooper, to join us. He was good friends with the band, which turned out perfect for us. During intermission he ran into Robby Krieger's girlfriend, Lynn, who gave him a ticket for the after-concert party. He was certain he could get all of us in and he did. Thank you, Michael.

Contrary to what some books have described, the after-party at the Forum was not all dark and gloomy. Actually, it was an excellent concert and Jim was in a good, even joking mood.

As for our first meeting, we locked eyes, smiled at each other, and the next thing I knew I'm in a quiet spot, away from the crowd, talking alone to Jim. We shared an instant attraction. What did we talk about? Nothing, everything, it was all very intense and very close.

I remember discussing the concert, complimenting him especially on how well he maneuvered and controlled an unruly audience—going from their demand to hear "Light My Fire" to the final performance of a well-staged poetic "Celebration of the Lizard." "Control?" Jim said, pausing for a moment, "No, I guided them."

I saw Jim a few weeks later at the Whisky (January 28, 1969) for a special Elektra Records press party for Delaney & Bonnie. I knew Delaney Bramlett from the *Shindig* TV show and was good friends with him and most of the band. Then Jim walked in with Ray and Robby. The place was so packed that even the label's top band couldn't get a seat and ended up sitting on the floor by the booths... right behind my table.

When the set was over I simply turned around and said, "Hi, Jim." I was going to remind him who I was, but he remembered my name, gave me a kiss on the cheek, and softly whispered in my ear, "You're going to go home with me, aren't you?" Just like that. Of course I said yes. I was very attracted to this man.

Actually, I didn't go home with Jim, he went home with me. My apartment was just a few blocks away, but it took us over an hour to walk there. We kept stopping to make out, if that's the best word for it. We made out in a phone booth, while Jim pretended to make a call. An alleyway was available, more kisses, then we sat on the sidewalk steps of someone's home, more touching, more foreplay. We didn't care. It was passionate, intense and completely uncharacteristic for me to act this way in public, but Jim made it fun and he certainly knew what he was doing.

Our romance began as a hot and heavy love affair, but after four or five months things cooled down, at least on his side. Not on mine. Life around Jim remained fascinating, the sex continued, but the sizzle gradually faded. "Friends with benefits" is an apt expression of what we slowly became— then just friends with shared interests, plans and friends in common. It was a comfortable relationship, and I figured things would continue like this for a long time to come, and then he went off to Paris.

Q: You also saw additional Doors concerts and Jim read poetry in public.

A: I was lucky to see several more Doors concerts, including both shows at the Aquarius, the San Francisco Cow Palace a few days later, and what would prove to be their final L.A. performance at the Long Beach Sports Arena.

But the best show I saw Jim perform wasn't with the band but at an event at the Cinematheque Theater on Sunset Boulevard. It was supposed to be a political fundraiser for Norman Mailer's New York mayoral campaign. Jim admired Mailer's literary accomplishments and his idealistic thoughts on politics and wanted to help his campaign.

The fundraiser turned into a party for Jim and his friends, actors and poets, Michael McClure, Seymour Cassell, Michael C Ford, Tom Baker and Mary Waronov, to celebrate what they loved best: movies, music and poetry. They screened the band's documentary film *Feast of Friends* and the guests recited their poetry and made some music. Two nights of just having fun, with a little audience participation thrown in. At one point Robby played guitar and Jim sang, just for the fun of it. Thankfully, some of the songs and poetry were recorded. Very special performances, but I don't think they raised much money.

I wrote a review of the performance for my column in *World Countdown* suggesting that Elektra put out a record featuring the poetry: "Perhaps this is a germ of something great to come. Doors concerts, mainly on college campuses, featuring movies, poetry and music." The Aquarius concert a few months later was the closest they ever came to it.

Q: Have the books on the Doors and Morrison told the story? Did the Oliver Stone–directed *The Doors* connect with you or get close to the truth? What did you think of his Doors film?

A: No matter how many books are written about the Doors and Jim Morrison, they will always get some things wrong—and some things right. I've only been interviewed a few times, and that was all over 20 years ago, except recently for a new documentary. I understand that it's impossible to get everything correct over time and memory. Life is subjective; so are authors. And so are readers.

One of the interviews I did was with Randall Jahnson for the first version of *The Doors* script. In Randall's script the group dynamics were stronger, especially dealing with Jim's conflicts and the poetic aspects that drove him. Oliver Stone's version of *The Doors* had its moments, especially the concert sequences, but sadly it never got close to capturing Jim's complex personality... especially his sense of humor, his Southern charm and his intelligence. Val Kilmer did get Jim's slow grin right, and his measured, soft-spoken speech pattern, but I felt the rest of the real Jim was lost. It was lost to Kilmer and to Stone. Jimbo starred in that movie and I don't know where the Jim I knew was.

The Jim I knew was extremely smart, sexy and mostly great fun to be around. He helped me decorate my Christmas tree one year and did a long monologue of sexual puns and innuendos about balls and other ornaments. How can you make icicles sexy? Jim could. I couldn't respond, I was laughing too hard.

Yes, Jim could get drunk and obnoxious at times, that's when Jimbo would come out to play. Luckily, I didn't see much of that, but when I did, it wasn't nice. We had a silly spat one night, one of those tests of wills that began over nothing in particular. Jim grew very quiet. He never yelled,

151

but got up and walked out without a word. It felt so final. He left me in tears and I figured we were over, but sure enough Jim came by a couple days later like nothing had happened. I felt we needed to say our apologies so I hesitantly brought it up. He didn't remember a thing. He said he was sorry and even apologized again when I saw him next. But Jim was apologizing for upsetting me, not for being shit-faced drunk. Only once did I ever see him yell at someone, scary, and I was glad it wasn't me.

Q: You discussed poetry with Jim?

A: I was impressed with Jim's poetry and I told him so. His choice of words was very careful, the words themselves offering a rhythm that matched the rhythm of the lines. No wonder some of his work made such outstanding lyrics. I still cherish my copy of his *American Prayer.*

But it was the piece he wrote for the October 1968 issue of *Eye Magazine* that intrigued me the most. His "rap," as the magazine called it, was about eyes—eyes everywhere—from the pineal gland, the third eye, the ancient lizard eye, "the jewel within their skull," the ancient Eye Temple of Brak, the symbol of the Egyptian God, Osiris, the Cyclops, alchemy, with eyes of light and eyes of the soul. He wove mysticism, history and religion into a fascinating piece of work. I wanted to know this man, not just interview him.

I hope *Eye Magazine* appreciated the irony about an article on eyes. I'm sure it was intentional, at least on Jim's part.

Q: Where did you go on dates? Restaurants? Movies? Did you go shopping for clothes? What was it like being with him?

A: INTENSE.

When Jim interacted with you, in any way, you had his complete attention. No distractions. Intense is the right word. Imagine a man who actually listens to everything you say. Very flattering.

Jim was interested in your opinion, but you had to be truthful. What did you really think? What did you like about a book, a song—or sex? That emotional ability to pull you into his world, to create a space for the two of you, it was wonderful. Raw, emotional, passionate. Of course I didn't want it to end.

Q: You noticed Jim had some medical problems.

A: Sometimes he had a wheezing chest congestion. Jim blamed it on smoking, but it wasn't until many years later I read that he had a problem with asthma. He never mentioned asthma to me, but I think it was in one of Frank Lisciandro's books. Jim did smoke, but wasn't a chain smoker who had to have a cigarette the moment he got out of bed. I don't smoke, but I was tolerant about it with friends in my home. Jim was considerate about his smoking and would sometimes go out on my patio to smoke, especially when smoking those odd-smelling cigarillo things that he liked.

Jim woke up one morning with a splitting headache. I gave him a massage and used some visualizing meditation techniques (a New Age version of an ancient Shamanic "talking cure" I knew about) to draw the pain out, gather it together and then throw it away. It worked. It's an easy meditation to do, but Jim wasn't interested in learning it. He knew about these techniques intellectually, but I think if he actually did them he'd have to admit that something was wrong.

Jim knew he drank too much, but he wouldn't admit to anyone, including himself, that drinking too much was actually a problem. It was, "I like to drink. I get drunk, no problem." Observed, mentioned, and then ignored.

Q: Where did you go on dates?

A: Jim and I had a lot in common when it came to background, sort of a cultural sensibility with a love of literature, music and many of the same social interests.

I think my apartment became a safe haven from outside distractions and responsibilities. I tried to make him comfortable, which I think I did especially after I figured out two things: always keep cold beer on hand, and it's OK to be quiet. Jim didn't need to be entertained.

Very few dates were planned in advance. We were more spontaneous and casual. After a night together we'd stop off at Duke's, a restaurant down the street, for a late lunch or we'd visit the Palms, his favorite bar near the Doors' office on Santa Monica Boulevard, which was only a few blocks away from my place.

As a music journalist I was out a lot, going to press events or reviewing one band or another at some clubs. Occasionally I'd bump into Jim, and we'd inevitably wind up together for the evening.

I was at Thee Experience one night to see my friend Spencer Davis perform. Though the club didn't last a year, it left behind some great stories that became rock 'n' roll legends. No drugs or sex-crazed orgies that night, just good music. Jim and I talked, had a drink or two, and after the show went back to my place. Typical of our relationship, no frills, no hassles, just a lot of talking, shared opinions and great sex.

Sometimes he would just show up with a late-night knock on my door or a phone call in the middle of the afternoon to see if I was available for lunch or some lovemaking—often with a side of anthropological chitchat thrown in (another favorite shared interest of ours). We were casual about the relationship, but it worked.

Q: Can you recall any film discussions you had with Jim?

A: I remember going to see *If...* with Jim at a small theater in Westwood. The film was directed by Lindsay Anderson and set in a British boys' school where the students were questioning authority and conformity, leading to a final conflict; chaos and confrontation, youth against power. The tagline was "Which side will you be on?" Jim loved it.

We enjoyed discussing movies. Jim was into foreign films a lot more than I was, but we had the same taste in many American movies. One of our favorites was *A Face in the Crowd*, about a charming con man who uses the media to become one of the most important, powerful people in America. *Ace in the Hole* and *A Lion Is in the Street* were among our favorites with similar themes.

Jim was always intrigued with the concept of being able to influence people, especially an audience. He knew he could do it, but he also realized that this ability to control was a double-edged sword. Jim was perfectly aware of how close chaos and power truly were. As he said in an interview, "Whoever controls the media controls the mind."

Jim also liked old black-and-white westerns including *Three Godfathers* as well as the classic old Universal horror movies, and he had seen most of the English Hammer films as well. He knew I loved horror movies.

Jim would read anything. He read *Vogue*, the *LA Free Press*, *World Countdown*, *Teen Screen*, *Flip* and anything else that might be sitting on my coffee table or stacked in my bookcases. That also included my early attempt at writing a novel about a rock band that makes it big, loses their way and then loses their lead singer. My fictional band was called Woodscolt. Wood's Colt is old Southern slang for a bastard. A work in progress, I had started it several years before and certainly didn't want anyone to read it at that stage, but Jim found it buried in a stack of notebooks.

The end of the novel was the lead singer's staged disappearance in a "lady or the tiger" style mystery. It was all plotted out so it could be a murder, suicide or a dramatic goodbye performance. Jim read some of it and gave me a few tips, especially how to write lyrics that really flowed. "Always read your writing out loud. That's the best way to edit." (Which is the same good advice my screenwriting teachers would later give.) But it was my ending that intrigued Jim the most, especially its ambiguity.

Instead of going through my record collection, which was almost a cliché for guests to do, he went straight for my book collection. At that time I hadn't even moved all of my books from my parents' house, but I had a good selection of ancient history, mythology, archaeology, comparative religion and lots of science fiction. I had a secondhand copy of *The Book of the Damned* by Charles Fort, a favorite of Jim's, plus a few books on UFOs and psychic phenomena. Jim enjoyed books.

Q: Jim was not preoccupied with money.

A: Jim usually carried his license and a credit card stuffed in his pants pocket, plus a few crumpled large bills. I think the Doors' office had accounts with several local places. But Jim always paid for everything. He didn't insist, he just did it, for me and for his other friends. Jim didn't seem to worry about money. It was useful. It had a purpose. He liked the travel and freedom it gave him, but money, and making a lot of money, was not a focus for him.

Q; In 1969, specifically after the infamous stage incident in Miami in Dade County, what were your concerns about his impending legal situation? I'm sure you were troubled by his plight.

A: I was at the Troubadour when I first heard about Jim and the Miami incident. I think Rodney Bingenheimer was the one who mentioned it to me. Some of my fellow music journalists hanging out in the bar had more details. By the time they were finished catching me up with the news and rumors, it sounded as if the police were chasing Jim practically through the Florida swamps with bloodhounds. Maybe that image wasn't far off as The Powers That Be were determined to take Jim Morrison down in the name of decency, their version of "decency."

The story about the Miami concert exploits grew and so did the lies. During the trial, so-called witnesses got up in front of a judge and jury, promised to tell the truth "so help me God" and flat-out lied. The truth was told, but it didn't make any difference in that moment of time. The politicians were determined to get a conviction in the name of decency, and they did. Those who played politics and lied under oath suffered no consequences, but that trial served as the catalyst—the beginning of the end for Jim. It devastated him. May they all rot in hell.

Q: Did you ever formally interview Jim?

A: Oddly enough, I never interviewed any of the Doors. Dave Marsh at *Creem* assigned me to interview Jim at one point, but we never got it done. The Doors' press agent, Leon Barnard, helped me with written materials, and even press photos from *Feast of Friends*, but the deadline was too close and schedules too tight at that point. I never did the interview. I know that would have been a great interview, a challenge, fun, but worth it. How I wish.

I have a note: "November 11, 1970—Saw Jim—looks great. Promised me a screening of his movie *HWY*." That's all I wrote down about *HWY* and I never did get a screening.

Q: And then Jim went to Paris.

A: I knew Jim wanted to get away from Los Angeles. He told me so months before he actually left, but at that time it was all speculation. He didn't make it sound as if he was really leaving to become an expat someplace. It sounded to me like he just wanted to get away from all of the responsibilities and entanglements in Los Angeles and the Miami trial. Jim needed to step away from everything for a while.

I saw Jim on March 2, 1971, and that's when he told me he was definitely heading to Paris and that he didn't plan to come back. The news was shocking to me, but understandable. We didn't discuss it further that day.

I saw him the following day at an Elektra party celebrating their new offices. The party was crowded, rather hectic and again no chance to really talk. I didn't see Jim again until early April. He was planning his trip and finishing *L.A. Woman* and I had just started a new job as national director of college promotion for United Artists/Liberty Records. We had so much to catch up on, but it was the trip to Paris I was most interested in.

I asked if he was still thinking about leaving for good. Yes, that was the plan, but maybe he'd return sometime, perhaps at the end of the summer. It all depended on so many outside factors. His life was up in the air and he wasn't in control. He said that really bothered him. The idea of living and writing in Paris sounded romantic, but getting away from the madness of Los Angeles was crucial.

He made me promise to call him early the following week before he left. He knew I didn't like to call the office except for business, but I promised I would. In a few days he'd be off to Paris and I'd be traveling on my first road trip back east for the record company. How things change.

We gave each other a long hug and a farewell kiss. Good luck. Keep in touch. Safe journey and all the usual wishes were exchanged. I know we both meant them. As we pulled away from each other, Jim said, "You'd better finish that rock novel of yours or I might steal the ending." That's exactly what he said. We both laughed. He gave me a final kiss on the cheek and walked away.

That was the last time I saw Jim Morrison.

PEACE

THE DOORS FAMILY

Doors Holiday Card Inside Envelope
Courtesy of Anne Moore

Tony Funches Interview, 2014

In the fall of 1969 I had a job in Culver City at the West Los Angeles Junior College library around a full schedule of classes. I also had a student deferment.

It was the first semester the college opened. We were taught in bungalows and would joke, "It's like a high school with ashtrays."

It was during that summer and fall of '69 that I made an acquaintance with a guy named Tony Funches, a Vietnam veteran, boxer and Karate belt holder, who soon became our student body president. Tony had been in Vietnam and I was sure making sure I wasn't gonna be going to that place. We had a few meals off the lunch truck and talked R&B and jazz when he came into the library.

But then I didn't see Tony on campus again during the last quarter of 1969 and all of 1970. I never knew why but found out later: Tony was newly employed at the time: serving as Mick Jagger's lone bodyguard on their '69 tour. In 1970 he would head security for the Doors and be Jim Morrison's minder and bodyguard.

Needless to say, when I first saw the documentary movie *Gimme Shelter* in 1970 with fellow classmate Bob Sherman in Hollywood, we immediately looked at each other when a somewhat familiar face initially appeared onscreen. First in a Muscle Shoals recording studio session during a playback of "Wild Horses" and then later protecting Jagger and the Stones around the group's airstream trailer in the madness engulfing Altamont. We both instantly marveled, "Hey—isn't that Tony from school?"

Yes, it was.

I am happy to say that in 2015 I reconnected with Tony Funches at the former 1967–68 home of Jim Morrison in Laurel Canyon.

Not from Facebook but owing to circumstances of destiny.

The Morrison residence was now owned by Matt King, a friend of Rob Hill, my editor at *THC Expose* magazine, who met Tony in Nevada. They had connected with Funches at a hotel bar and mentioned my name. Phone calls were made and arrangements by Hill and King for Tony to come to Los Angeles were done.

When I arrived to the rustic scene of many rhymes, Tony and I warmly embraced. He had a copy of my *Canyon of Dreams: The Magic and Music of Laurel Canyon* and wanted me to autograph it.

I subsequently interviewed Tony for three hours, with Rob and Matt in attendance, followed by a meal at Barney's Beanery. Shortly afterwards John Densmore came by the house and drove Tony off.

Q: How did you even get into security work?

A: I got out of the Air Force in very late 1968 and it started with a guy named Donnie Branker and West Coast Productions.

Q: You met the Stones in 1969 after doing some local security work at music concerts.

A: I didn't have any preconceived notions about them, but my perception of all these folks was still based from living in Crenshaw Village, the projects, the black part of Los Angeles and coming up there.
    Most of the hang and the relationship were based on their personalities turning out to be likable. Otherwise I'd go back to what I was doin' before I met them.

Q: You had already been in Vietnam and in jungle wars, seeing friends of your shot in a river.

A: The world of personal security was a new world for me. Absolutely. I didn't see it that way. I still saw myself as a Vietnam vet, a student body president at WLAJC, getting a degree, and the expectations of the family, and these other folks just paying me dough to do this, that and the other was laughable. At first I thought it was a joke. They can't be serious.
    But my primary view of myself at the time was that I dropped out of school long enough to do this tour and I would have enough cash to stash and wouldn't have to sweat the next semester. It was $75 a week. This is 1969.

161

At the time I quit the Stones three times on the '69 tour. "Fuck you, bunch of skinny white boys! Kiss my black ass. I quit. I'm the fuck outta here." Other people in their entourage got big for their britches and pissed me off.

Q: As you look back at the Altamont situation, give me a reflection. You had already been in Vietnam. Maybe that is one of the reasons you survived.

A: You are not reading too much into it, but the insanity of violence doesn't change whether it's Vietnam, Altamont or the inner city. Rural or urban. It doesn't make any difference. Bullies and events will kill other human beings for no reason. Yes, did it happen at Altamont? Yes. It happened in the whole neighborhood.

Q: But I remember you from college. A serious student, a Vietnam vet, student body president who knew about planning and execution. You were way older than us teenagers, as you went to school on the G.I. Bill.

A: I knew about chaos. I told 'em. I saw it comin' way way far in advance. I told a couple of people, and they said, "That's not what we pay you for." I was lookin' out. "Do what we pay you for and it will be fine." "OK."

Altamont was in December '69, I got maybe a week off, and I turned 21 on January 17, 1970, and then the Doors hired me and I was in Madison Square Garden with the Doors.

I saw the show in New York and said, "Toto. I don't think this is Kansas anymore." The Doors at the Felt Forum compared to the Stones at Madison Square Garden a month earlier was a walk in the park. Some kid during the opening song, fried on acid, or Lords knows what, just slithered like a snake up and over the stage barrier and coiled himself around Jim's microphone stand. And I went to remove him

162

and Siddons gave me a hi sign and the kid, a young guy, he stayed like a snake in a perfect coil around Jim's mike stand throughout the entire set.

I was home for maybe three weeks after Altamont and the Stones until the Doors. I had been with the Stones at Madison Square Garden in November of '69.

I liked the music of the Doors, but they were so different from any and everything and anybody I had ever experienced before that it took some getting used to. They're both good but no way similar. Far too disparate to be spoken in the same breath.

Q: What were your first impressions in meeting the Doors?

A: Really mellow and intelligent white boys. Seriously. Conversations that occurred were intelligent. They had the presence of mind not to talk down. Because then they wouldn't have had nobody to take the job or I walk my black ass out the door, motherfuckers. They spoke as grown and intelligent men to another grown and intelligent man. In the course of our brief conversation conspicuously and consciously created an atmosphere of relaxed discourse. And I grabbed that and everything was cool.

The total of the Doors concert experience was so permeating in its competency, originality and adulthood, fascinating intellectuality in all aspects. It was completely new and revolutionary to me but being a jazz aficionado could dig it on that level plus during that previous time when they hired me and we actually went to New York to do the gig we had had by then many discussions about Elvin Jones and Oscar Peterson. But they were really happy I was a jazz fan as well.

I was thinking to myself, "You fuckin' idiots. I'm from South Central L.A. [Laughs.] I'm black, my family does jazz, has been since before you were born; why are you surprised I know jazz, man?" White folks are weird. By then we were all firing on the same cylinders because we're all jazz freaks. It's not the big black guy and little white boys. It's all these jazz fans. See? And that was the cohesive force as it were.

Robby Krieger. I respected Robby for his virtuosity with flamenco and classic guitar. And he shit a green biscuit when I ran Django Reinhart passed him. I'd been a fan of music for quite a long time going back to being a kid at the black newspaper. *The Eagle.*

John Densmore. John is a good guy. John was the constant nanny reminding everybody they were supposed to behave. Ray and Robby behaved, and the only two left to behave were me and Jim. And Jim used to do shit just to aggravate John. Playfully, brother to brother. Right? And I hung with Jim but John always appreciated how well I did my job. I was a minder for the Doors and worked closer with Jim. As in anything it is always an ever-changing landscape. It's my job, whether it be the Stones or the Doors, Waylon or Willie, all of 'em, if you're a bodyguard or a road or tour manager, a lot of the time I did all three at the same time, wasn't limited to the intellectuality of busted knuckles.

Ray Manzarek was my bud. He had been in the military like me. I was always grateful we could escape any scenario where Ray had to sing. So was he and so was everybody else. Love the guy. Ray wasn't so much a disciplinarian. He did the same thing that I did when we were putting the student government together when we were at West Los Angeles College. He listened to all the different points and would repeat all that back to the opposing forces that would then agree to what he said. That was Ray's talent, and he had a degree in economics.

I could actually compute a box office settlement and do percentages on the break point after thirty-two five after you take out sound and lights and the allowances for the agency and advertisements. I was a responsible person given the areas of responsibility and that's based on the perception of that person of what the responsibility is. If I'm wearing the tour manager hat but if I notice something that affects the long-term best interest of the band with the press, but I'm watching out for my employer.

And Vince Traynor, who did the Doors' equipment, he built it and took it all apart, you'll never see the likes of again. Amps, speakers, he more than the task of driving crystal-clear studio sound through the biggest venues they played, and Jim with his sense of humor, knowing how idiosyncratic Vince was about that equipment, Jim quite often would tape his vocal microphone and stick it in the PA so the defect was cracking windows and people's ear drums just to watch Vince get demonized of daggers because Vince was fucking with his talents. How glamorous is it to have an article about a tech-freak mad scientist that built a sound system the likes of which no one will ever see again. And nobody knew how it worked! How he'd do it? He didn't tell nobody what he did.

Jim had his scene down. An apartment on West Norton Avenue, the Doors' office, the Alta Cienega motel, and Elektra Records on Santa Monica Boulevard and La Cienega Boulevard. All stumbling distance from each other. [Laughs.] All within two or three blocks.

At the *L.A. Woman* sessions they were having fun. It was a whole different vibe than the informal formality of being at the Elektra studio or Sunset Sound because they were so at home there downstairs, which was essentially their rehearsal room. When they decided to do the album there, here's ol' Vince and he wasn't, and we could all tell, wasn't really elated to have them record there because nobody knows where Vince got the knowledge.

Some people are idiot savants. But the idea of them recording there doing *L.A. Woman* allowed him and them to fully employ all those things that he knew he could do and of

165

course of them recording. All the equipment that he had taken apart and modified was in the same room with the Doors downstairs and now he's gonna configure the room to work with the equipment that he built. So he stepped into his own element in the process of them recording there, Vince, I think, in that current was able to do his masterwork expression, as it were. And I think the sound of *L.A. Woman* reflects Vince's contribution.

Q: You were at the Doors' office in April 1970 and saw Jim Morrison's *The Lords and the New Creatures* when a box of poetry books arrived.

A: I had a copy Jim autographed and gave to me but I lost it. Yeah… That was so cool. That was so fuckin' cool. On that particular day I had no specific real duties to perform other than I just happened to be there. Jim was really excited. Everybody was. All of his bandmates and all of the Doors family, as it were, just really happy for him. An incredible festive moment that wasn't real done in a formal sense. The cases of the books arrived and everybody went, "Hey, Jim. Your books are here." Low-key. Jim was like real shy about opening it up and he was trying to hide how proud he was because this was a step to legitimacy as a poet, and after we opened the first case of books, everyone said, "Fuck it, man, let's party." I thoroughly enjoyed the occasion of seeing him that happy. Unbridled pure happiness. Not with sticking his chest out getting all stupid, the quiet happiness of seeing oneself validated. So that was so fuckin' special.

I know that there was some drama in Simon & Shuster finally winding up as the publisher. There was intense drama associated with that. After I signed on was when the Doors and Jim had found out they had been accepted by ASCAP.

Unlike BMI, you have to petition to ask and join. There is a board of governors or a membership votes on

166

whether to accept your money ass, right? Acceptance into ASCAP was huge. When Jimmy and the Doors got accepted into ASCAP it was total elation. Jim was really a humble guy and almost apologetically so. He cared about such things that others would recognize if not his talent his efforts to be an artist. That's why the Lizard King, bullshit teenybopper shit drove him up the wall.

Q: The Doors and Albert King played the Long Beach Arena in 1970.

Ticket Stub
Courtesy of Ida Miller

A: I went to get Jim for the show. He was staying at the Alta Cienega. When I knocked on the door, he said he was working on a poem and he would be at the concert... I believed him, and a few minutes before the concert, up pulls a cab and Jim is in it.

Jim had the artistic bent that allowed him, given his rebelliousness and the idiom he was expressing himself through, to do that improvisation in live performances or on records. He did that in his artistic expressions because that capability was resident within his personality. While at the same time he drew comfort in knowing that others had been doing similar things, as with Cab Calloway doing scat singing with the zoot suit or Bobby Darin when he did "Mack the Knife." So he knew of those things, but he did not do them as they did, but he was aware that others had improvised

167

similarly, and since they had, he figured, "I'm gonna give it a try. But I can't do what they do." So he did what he did according to what made him tick, which made it separate but not equal. But separate.

It wasn't up to me to be Jim's nanny. You could influence him as best you can. If Jim decided to get stoned or stinkin' drunk before a gig, sometimes I could head that off and other times... I didn't live with the cat for 24/7, ya know. I was at home in Venice. He's gonna do what he was gonna do. We did a little bit of telephone, had meals. We both ate meat and potatoes. He had a house as well on Kings Road. I went there once or twice. The mysterious house that he got into for tax purposes. He had a few crates and boxes.

One time I went with Jim to see his accountant, Bob Greene. The Doors were protected. They completely managed themselves. But they had extra advice from excellent people. Jim really didn't see himself as a participatory mogul in the business of the Doors. But since he had come up with the idea of it being a democracy, at certain times he had to show up and participate. It was his idea, and he couldn't very well just say, "You guys go ahead, I'll sit it out." And they'd remind him of that. "You gotta show up." As soon as he could weasel out of the official duties, he'd say, "Come on, man, let's go get a drink over at the Phone Booth." He did say one time, "I'm now involved in an avocado farm," or an almond farm. He never carried cash. The accountant always made sure I had five grand.

Jim could be so comical. Kind of like a kid. He had his Diners Club card. He had two or three credit cards and he got in the habit of remembering to carry them. And he used them exclusively. All of those transactions went straight to his accountant's office, who took care of them. Jim never knew how much money he had. He was a millionaire and didn't know it.

Q: You were in Dade County, Miami, in 1970 for Morrison's trial, where he was charged with a felony count of lewd and lascivious behavior and indecent exposure, when the guilty verdict was read. In 2011, the outgoing governor Charlie Crist pardoned Jim Morrison in the indecent-exposure case against him.

A: I didn't agree with the original verdict, for a crime that he didn't commit. In spite of the fact that they knew constitutionally that he was innocent. And that they knew that he never actually did what he was charged with. Even if it was theatrical expression, he still never did it. But it was expedient to the powers that be in the oligarchy to prosecute and persecute because he was already then an icon available to folks who might care to think freely and independently outside of the media noise. So he was aware of the ludicrous comicality of that.

Max Fink and Paul Josephson were the lawyers. Sharp as a motherfucker. Tall cat. Younger than Max. Paul took the tactical lead and it wasn't until Max had some point he wanted to make. The whole thing was a ludicrous kangaroo court. And the U.S. press were compliant with the government and giving any credibility to the trial and the charges. When the same thing happens to other artists in other countries, the press chimes in that it's a kangaroo court and a monkey trial... But they chose not to where Jimmy was concerned. And thus gave the trial judicial legitimacy. I was under orders from Leon [Barnard] Siddons and Ray and everybody else to keep my comments private. But they and the band Jim all knew my opinions.

Q: Was he scared?

A: Not really scared but thoroughly concerned, yes. Doing time in the slam was something I had to consider.

169

Q: You knew pretty early that Jim was planning to go to Paris.

A: Jim asked me many times if he should go to Paris. As he said, he was just looking forward to the whole European vibe, and sincerely as a friend he said, "It's OK, Tony. I'll be fine. It's different there."

Then I got the news. I got a little groggy. I feel good when I hear a Doors song. Their place in history at least thus far is assured.

Bruce Botnick Interview, 2014

Los Angeles native Bruce Botnick is a sound engineer and record producer. At age 18 he talked his way into a job at Liberty Records in Hollywood where he subsequently recorded Bobby Vee, Johnny Burnette, Jackie DeShannon, Leon Russell and David Gates, with arranger Jack Nitzsche.

Botnick then moved to Sunset Sound, hired as a mixer initially to do children's albums for Disney.

Then the Doors walked in off the street into the fabled Sunset Sound facility with their producer, Paul A. Rothchild, an A&R signing courtesy of Elektra Records' founder and owner, Jac Holzman.

Botnick is acclaimed for engineering the entire Doors recording catalogue as well as engineering Love's first two albums. He also produced their seminal *Forever Changes* LP in 1967. He co-produced the Doors' *L.A. Woman.*

Bruce was at the dials at several epic rock 'n' roll special moments: "Here Today" from Brian Wilson's *Pet Sounds*, Buffalo Springfield's "Blue Bird" and "Expecting to Fly," and a credit as an assistant engineer to Glyn Johns on the "Gimme Shelter" session on the Rolling Stones' *Let It Bleed.*

In 1996 Ray Manzarek introduced me to Bruce inside his Beverly Hills home one afternoon. "Botnick, meet Kubernik."

Q: So many incredible albums were recorded at Sunset Sound in Hollywood on Sunset Boulevard. Love, Doors, Buffalo Springfield, the Rolling Stones mixed *Beggars Banquet* and *Exile on Main Street* in the facility.

Tell me about the studio and the magic of the atmosphere.

A: It was built by a man named Alan Emig, who had come from Columbia Records. He was a well-known mixer there and designed a custom-built 14-input tune console for Sunset Sound.

Salvador "Tutti" Camarata, a trumpet player originally and an arranger, and did big band stuff in the 1940s and '50s, had a friendship with Disney and decided to build a recording studio to handle the Disney records and all the movies, *20,000 Leagues Under the Sea*. On a normal day we'd go from 8:00 a.m. to 9:30 p.m. with commercials.

Q: You worked a bit earlier with arranger and musician Jack Nitzsche on records by Bobby Vee and Jackie DeShannon.

A: He came into the picture early on when I was doing work for Liberty Records, which is where I came from. Jack was the arranger on a Bobby Vee date. Jack was the arranger and liked what he heard. He had been working over at RCA and at Gold Star doing a lot of recording. He started bringing tons of stuff in.

And right in the middle of that relationship with Jack, the Doors walked through the door. I had already done Love before that. And the Doors came in the door with Paul [Rothchild]. Knowing that in between the first Love album and

171

the first Doors album was the first Tim Buckley album. And that was the first album that Paul Rothchild had done since he had gotten out of jail for a trumped-up government charge on marijuana, where they had sent him stuff in the mail. And he opened the box. "My goodness. Look at this. Where did this come from?" And the next thing was the doorbell rang and there was the Drug Enforcement Agency.

Q: At Sunset Sound, what did the room bring to the recordings you engineered or produced?

A: Well, the room was very unique. Tutti Camarata did something that nobody had done in this country. He built an isolation booth for the vocals. And later on I convinced him to take the mono disc mastering system and move it into the back behind what became Studio 2. And we turned that into a very large isolation booth, which we used to put strings in. That's one of the things that worked so well for Jack Nitzsche, because we were able to put six strings in there and get full isolation live. It was great.

With the stings being in the large isolation booth, the drums didn't suffer, so we were able to make tighter and punchier rhythm tracks than any of the other studios in town were able to do. 'Cause everybody did everything live in those days. You did your vocals live. You did your strings and your brass live. And the rhythm section. And this was a big deal. And then add to it the amazing echo chamber that Alan Emig designed. Still phenomenal and having survived a fire. It still sounds incredible.

Microphones and placement. All different microphones have different coloration and different sounds. And, if you have a good selection, like we did at Sunset Sound, it was all tubes, except for some Ribbon, RCA's and a few Dynamics, they were all tube microphones. U-47s, Sony.

And we picked the microphone depending on the sound we were trying to get. And that was part of the palate. I still take that approach to this day. And by choosing the right microphone and putting it in the right place, a lot of times you can avoid having to EQ it.

Q: Did you ever employ windscreens, foam items or a pop filter to for vocal performances?

A: I did not do that. I could hear the change in the vocal quality and I didn't like it. So what I did is, I got a couple of singers stoned by making my own windscreens out of stockings and gluing them onto frames that I built, so they would be smelling the vapors of the model glue. But that worked great as a pop filter and did not affect the quality of vocals very much. I built things that went around the microphones, and I have seen photographs from Capitol and they did the same thing.

Q: Do you feel you obtained a different or even better sound recording in your initial '60s sessions partially to the restrictions of 3- and 4-track machines and not 8, 16 or 24 tracks for basic recording? Although by the album *Strange Days* the Doors were using 8-track.

A: Yes, I believe that by making those decisions and getting that sound and printing it. The great thing about it, if you wind up working on it and overdubbing vocals or whatever, the other stuff never changes. It stays in that same place. What you heard that first time when you locked it in, it's there. Now, that can be done with modern technology and I do it all the time when I do movie scores. Where we shoot everything live. I print all the automation, all the EQ, reverbs. It's all done. So when I have to come in and do a mix or a remix, by adding electronics to it, or melding all the other

173

stuff that I work against is still locked. Even though I have full breakout capabilities. So I still maintain that same process to this day.

Q: What kind of recording tape did you generally use on sessions?

A: It was Scotch 111. The Scotch tape, first off, you could kill it, and today it still plays. The oxide is still on the backing. A lot of the later low-noise tapes that happened, especially with Ampex and some Scotch 207, the oxide turned to mush due to the backing and the glue. And we always had a problem with Ampex tape until near the end. With the bottom end that it almost sounded grainy. You couldn't get a good, clear bass note. On some basses that was good because it made it sound a little crunchier. But generally the favored tape was Scotch.

L.A. had a lot of great studios at one time. United Recording Studios, Western Recorders, Gold Star, Sunset Sound, RCA. They were terrific rooms. There was a commonality between them. They all had the same loud speakers, which were Altec Lansing 604s. So you could walk from studio to studio and know what the hell you were hearing. Some rooms had more bottoms than others. But still the general, overall sound was the same. So you could take your tape and go to another room.

Q: What is it like birthing a recording, then following it over the decades in the transfer process from vinyl, to cassette, to the digital world, CD, and now Blu-ray.

A: I can tell you something. The machines we had then to record on recorded better than they played back. And we are able today, much better playback, electronics better, and much better matching of the electronics to the heads. And I have been able to pull off the tapes much better sound than

I had ever heard. More bottom end. More openness in the air. Then work on it in that space and then mix it down to whatever it is we are putting out. If we're putting out a new Blu-ray, that's what it becomes. Or even stereo. It starts better at the higher sampling rates, and if you can keep it there, all the better.

Like, when I mastered the Doors albums for vinyl. Because some of the tapes were in fragile condition, I very carefully transferred them over, did any cleanup that needed to be done, and then we mastered right from that to vinyl. And those discs sound better to me than the originals we did back in the late '60s and early '70s. They are just more open. We're not doing some of the bad things we used to do in those days. More frequency crossover so that you could put more level on the disc. We were more concerned and more interested today in capturing on what was on the tape and putting it on the record than going for a level. Because we're not playing it on the radio anymore.

Q: What astounds you 40, 45 years later listening to your collaboration with Paul Rothchild and the Doors?

A: The thing that still works for me is, first and foremost, the music. The musicianship. The performance. And all of those when these guys connected as a unit and became unconscious is good or better than anything I've ever heard. I was just working on a score that I had recorded with Jerry Goldsmith on a movie called *First Night*. And it's extraordinary because a good half of the album the 110 musicians were totally unconscious and the performances spectacular. And that's one of the things I have to hand to my friend, producer Paul Rothchild. That we went for performance and tried to stay out of it not to become too technically in the front of the albums that were manufactured.

In the case of the Doors, Paul was the man who drove the train and kept it on the tracks. But the reality is that there were six of us in the studio making these records together. And it wasn't a matter of one person being "the person." Paul never took that point. At some point during the relationship and especially when Jim got busted in Miami, where Paul had to step up and take more control. Because somebody had to or otherwise it would have never got done. But generally his approach was to get the performance. And we weren't afraid of editing between takes. You get an amazing first verse and second verse and a chorus and verse into the bridge and it would sort of fall apart and we would grab another take that had it and edited it all together. And it was about the performance. It wasn't about overdubbing. Because in the majority of what the Doors played on their records was played live.

Q: Just before the album *L.A. Woman* formally began, Rothchild leaves the project. When you became a producer on *L.A. Woman*, after being the engineer previously on their sessions, is it true you brought in Presley's bassist, Jerry Scheff, to motivate or make Jim Morrison comfortable in the recording studio?

A: That's partially true. I brought Jerry in because I had just done an album, him playing on Mark Benno's solo album. So, I thought, "Gee, guys. How 'bout if I bring in Jerry Scheff. Oh, by the way, he's Elvis Presley's bass player." And Jim thought, "Wow. That's cool. I like that. I love Elvis." Then I suggested to Robby, "What would you think about bringing in a rhythm guitar into some of the songs so you'd be free and not have to do any overdubbing?" He said, "I like that a lot." 'Cause he always had to do his rhythm part and then play his solos separately.

It was done at the Doors' rehearsal space. Not Sunset Sound or Elektra. We just wanted to get it on tape. Going again for performance and not trying to be too perfect. Go for a little bit more raw approach.

You have to realize that when Buffalo Springfield came into the studio, they were rehearsed. They had played their music live. Double sets at nightclubs. Same thing as the Doors. That's one of the reasons we were able to get good performances.

Q: Can we talk about Elektra Records founder Jac Holzman?

A: I will tell you that Jac is the last of a long line of special people in the record business who did it, their total reason, their total reason for being in the music business was the music. The fact that they made money, the old-fashioned way, was because of their passion for the music.

It was music first and they knew it was right and if people responded they would get the money. It wasn't like the music today where the focus is on making the quarterly numbers.

Jac's taste in music was eclectic. What he did can be done today. It just takes somebody with strong musical tastes and a belief and a passion to do it. And build this. He is being inducted into the Rock and Roll Hall of Fame. Long overdue. I miss Ahmet, I miss even Clive Davis in his early years. Because he had a vision and really turned Columbia Records around into what it became. All these guys. That was the record business. Right now there is no record business and it's because there aren't people with vision and really a true passion for the music running it.

Rob Hill interview with Daveth Milton, 2017

Rob Hill 2017 interview with **Daveth Milton**, author of *We Want the World: Jim Morrison, the Living Theatre and the FBI*. Bennion Kearny Limited. April 27, 2012.

RH: First off, fascinating book. Just a great read for any Doors/Morrison fan. Give us a quick snapshot of your background and what led you to this interesting project. Were you always a Doors fan?

DM: My own background is academic. I studied the culture of popular music internationally at university before I started *We Want the World*. In fact, I had written a manuscript on a different musician. A prominent publisher told me my chosen subject, at that point, was just too well behaved to warrant a book, so I had a rethink. My mind turned to those iconic figures of the 1950s and 1960s, people like James Dean and Janis Joplin. Jim Morrison always struck me as the most fascinating of that group of people. He was a contrary figure, but behind his rebellion lay immense creativity and some interesting ideas.

Q: How did you get access to the 92 pages on Morrison in the FBI files? Tell us about this process.

A: I started researching *We Want the World* in the mid-1990s. There was little on the internet back then to speak of. When I read about Jim, I figured out that other biographers had obtained his FBI file but not made much of it. If they could get hold of it, I reasoned, so could I. So I wrote to the FBI asking them to send me the file under the Freedom of Information Act. They obliged. In fact, I collected a few FBI files of famous musicians back then, but the process became very slow.

Q: When and how did J. Edgar Hoover first realize Morrison was a threat to the establishment? And what actions did he take? Did they ever meet?

A: The first firm date we have for Hoover hearing about the Doors is March 20, 1969. He received a press clipping about the infamous Dinner Key concert from an ex-FBI field agent who ran a chain of radio stations. Local FBI agents in Miami evidently registered their concern about two weeks earlier, but we cannot be sure that Hoover personally was privy to their report. His first response was to express his disgust to the man who sent the clipping. Morrison was under the Bureau's jurisdiction in less than a week after Hoover read the clipping, with a warrant out for his arrest. In that sense, J. Edgar Hoover and Jim Morrison evidently had a hostile meeting of minds. The FBI leader was "bad father" to Jim's rebellious son. Both loved America. Each had conflicting views about it. They never met in person, but their entanglement amounted to a riveting spectacle—a kind of psychic car crash that deserved more attention in the space of writing. I wanted to call the book a "metaphysical thriller," but my publisher thought that might confuse people!

Q: You spend a good amount of time looking into how the Living Theatre, and its founder, Julian Beck, had a big influence on Morrison and what eventually happened in Miami. What was Beck's relationship like with Jim?

A: Together with his partner Judith Malina, Julian Beck acted out a much more direct threat to the American establishment than Jim, but on a smaller scale. Their anarchist troupe the Living Theatre aimed to reinvent society by using performance as a laboratory: doing things like burning money onstage. Like punk a few years later, such acts provoked a violent response. Malina even had her hair set on fire. Beck and Malina became an important part of my book because their productions—particularly *Paradise Now*—enacted the radicalism that Jim gestured toward in popular music. Morrison was their friend because he was, ideologically, one of their allies. They met up in San Francisco, just after the Doors' Miami concert. Jim offered $2,500 to fund their operation.

Q: You cover a VERY important 6 weeks in Morrison and the Doors career: From January 24, when they played Madison Square Garden, to March 1, when Miami happened. Can you talk in detail about this time frame? What was Morrison up to?

A: The "Wishful Sinful" single was released early in February. Jim was also arrested in L.A. for driving drunk without a license. Toward the end of the month, together with Michael McClure and manager Bill Siddons, he spent five nights attending the Living Theatre's University of Southern California shows. He even took their advance man, Mark Amitin, out to dinner. On the first night, he saw *Mysteries and Smaller Pieces*, which included a performance of Antonin Artaud's *Plague*, a piece that used taboo images to shock spectators awake: the actors walked among the audience and "died" of plague. Others came to take away their bodies, piling them up as if in a holocaust. Some people speculate the Doors' *Rock Is Dead* session might have taken place the day after that performance. The next two nights saw a production of *Frankenstein* where the monster was made by an acrobatic composite of cast members. *Frankenstein* asked whether a society born in violence could ever survive without it. At the show's climax, troupe members were individually arrested. After that, Morrison saw the Living Theatre's production of the Greek tragedy *Antigone*, a play which showed how civic leaders could face a gruesome comeuppance if they ignored their citizens' humanity.

On their final night at USC, the troupe put on their most infamous set piece, *Paradise Now*. Its start was delayed by half an hour due to disputes over fire safety and advanced payment. *Paradise Now* was about enacting a release from social conformity by the crossing of borders. Usually, the cast went naked as part of the protest, but they toned it down that night at USC. Even so, the whole night teetered on the edge of a riot and LAPD surrounded the building with 40 police cars. It was a real inspiration for Jim, and definitely helped to shape his thinking about the possibilities liberating people through interactive performance.

Q: Can you talk a little bit about who Lawrence Mahoney is?

A: Mahoney was a staff writer at the *Miami Herald* who took on the role of moral entrepreneur after the Dinner Key concert. He painted Jim Morrison as an agent of chaos who had failed in his mission. Mahoney's stories departed quite a long way from objectivity in their efforts to stir up trouble. The titles said it all. "Rock Group Fails to Stir a Riot" was Mahoney's initial, pivotal account. That was followed by "Public Reacts to Rock Show," "Disgrace at Dinner Key" and "Grossed Out by the Doors." Mahoney then chronicled the events he had set in train: "Rock Singer Charged," "Too Much Restraint Shown in Doors Case," "Singer Jim Morrison Guilty of Indecency" and, most ominously, "Morrison and Miami: Beginning of the End." We have to remember that there were police in the security staff at the Dinner Key event, and nobody much minded what happened. Mahoney was not satisfied. He used a notion of public decency to enlist the *Herald*'s readership and hold the local police to account, writing that "at no time was any effort made by the police to arrest Morrison." Local police then had to respond.

Q: How did the FBI react right after the Miami incident?

A: The local branch of the FBI internally reported the Miami show as part of COINTELPRO, the Bureau's catchall counterintelligence program. It then explored securing a felony charge for Morrison, something that would prevent him walking away, salvage the public reputation of the Dade County police and allow the Bureau to get involved in Jim's extradition case. That was a masterstroke of politics by means of law enforcement.

Q: At one point, was Morrison really a fugitive?

A: "Fugitive from justice" is a legal description applied to anyone involved in "unlawful flight to avoid prosecution." In other words, by itself, it can criminalize an individual, or at least add an extra charge against anyone who is already facing prosecution. For the FBI the term was, in part, a publicity tool: It clearly defined anyone designated as such as a villain. The Bureau was chasing 19,000 fugitives in 1969, using the label as part of its mission to gain publicity from stamping out crime.

Jim's legal designation as a fugitive came almost a month after his infamous supposed exposure incident at the Dinner Key Auditorium near Miami. On March 27 U.S. Commissioner Edward P. Swan issued a fugitive warrant that squarely placed Morrison's case within the remit of the FBI. I surmise in the book that the Bureau may actually have intervened to make that happen when, ordinarily, the impulse has to come from local police who request FBI involvement.

What the Bureau didn't bank on was that Morrison found out about his designation in less than three days. He visited a local FBI field office on April 3 and was bailed for $5,000. It took until April 24, however, for the Assistant U.S. Attorney to drop the fugitive charge. The warrant's slow repeal indicated how much wishful thinking (and perhaps bureaucracy) there was at FBI. Threats to the establishment were easier to address if they were designated as criminal matters; the Bureau wanted Morrison labeled a fugitive because the designation suited its tactics.

Q: Talk a little bit about Jim's lawyer, Max Fink. Did he serve Jim well? What was their relationship like?

A: Fink was a Beverly Hills attorney of considerable experience who was recommended to the band by Robby Krieger's father. He was much older than his clients and did his best for them. He and Jim were friends to the extent that they escaped on holiday to the Bahamas together in 1970. I think that Fink had a lot to handle when he took on Jim Morrison. Apparently Jim seduced his lady friend and also walked out of at least one of their meetings. But Fink was, evidently, very professional. He was skilled at preventing things from blowing up and getting to court, putting in appeals, and filing for retrials. He was also good at playing witnesses off against each other. Fink never made Morrison untouchable, but Morrison could have done much worse.

Q: What was then-governor of California Ronald Reagan's connections to Morrison and the FBI?

A: Fink had a connection to Reagan through a mutual friend. He thought he might persuade Reagan to speak to the right people and prevent things coming to court in regard to Morrison's infamous exposure incident. The problem was that Reagan was a better friend of the FBI. Back in the 1950s, he had infiltrated the Screen Actors Guild and exposed potential communists. Once he found out about Jim's reputation, Reagan sent Fink an apology. Jim had to return to Dade County and turn himself in at the Public Safety Department. In terms of subsequent history, it would have been very ironic, however, if Ronald Reagan had—a few years prior to his presidency— been the man who rescued Jim Morrison.

Q: How did the FBI react to Morrison being arrested in November 1969 on a plane heading to Arizona to see the Rolling Stones?

A: Morrison and his friend Tom Baker's drunken, childish pranks inconvenienced the other passengers and divided the captain's attention. They used bad language and maintained a defiant attitude. Some witnesses felt threatened. The Bureau seized upon the incident as a new opportunity to nail Morrison. Because it happened onboard an aircraft, agents knew the case was within their jurisdiction. On the same day that Morrison and Baker were bailed, Hoover sent a memo direct from Washington joining the dots. The "intimidation of a flight crew" charge carried a sentence of up to a decade in jail. In addition to that, they knew such a serious accusation would likely influence the trial about to happen in Miami. The FBI thought it could use Morrison's drunken pranks as a means of taking him out of the picture.

Q: When Jim said he was having a nervous breakdown in December 1969, how much do you think the FBI and the law targeting him had to do with that?

A: Rather a lot... given the breakdown came about a month after the Phoenix incident, when Jim still had to face both the Phoenix and Miami prosecutions. He had just missed his first hearing in Phoenix, which was not a good idea. It is also indicative that Jim had the breakdown in the Doors' L.A. office, as if it was connected with his public role.

Q: Do you think Morrison's paranoia and fear of going to jail and being hounded by the FBI contributed to his death in Paris? Do you think he died of "natural" causes?

A: In terms of the first question, I would say yes. Those things created a personal trauma that stressed Jim out, even if at times he looked like he ignored them. As we know, people under immense stress do not always look after their health too well.

To answer the second question, I really do not know how Jim died. It would be tempting to entertain different theories, but as much as possible, I based *We Want the World* purely on known facts from reliable sources. The book's narrative plausibly connects some dots but deliberately refrains from tipping over into conspiracy.

THE DOORS ELECTRIFY ON SCREEN AND STAGE WITH *WHEN YOU'RE STRANGE* SOUNDTRACK
RecordCollectorNews.com, 2010

Rhino celebrates the Doors' legacy as one of America's most influential rock bands with a soundtrack to coincide with the theatrical release of *When You're Strange: A Film About the Doors*, the first feature documentary about the Doors.

When You're Strange delivers an intimate look at the Doors using previously unseen footage filmed between 1965 and 1971. Produced by Wolf Films/Strange Pictures, in association with Rhino Entertainment, and released by Abramorama, the 90-minute documentary is written and directed by Tom DiCillo and narrated by Johnny Depp.

The soundtrack contains selections of Jim Morrison's poetry as read by Depp, 14 songs that survey the Doors' six landmark albums, with original studio versions of classic tracks ("Touch Me," "The End," and "L.A. Woman") along with rare live performances from *The Ed Sullivan Show* ("Light My Fire"), Danish TV ("When the Music's Over"), and the Isle of Wight Festival ("Break On Through [To the Other Side]"). The set also incorporates interview clips with all four band members.

Filmmaker DiCillo offers, "The Doors' music is the rock equivalent to film. It has great drama, sex, poetry, and mystery. Their music is for all those who've ever felt the cool chill of isolation and oddness in themselves; which in effect is all of us."

"I'm stunned how gorgeous the *HWY* footage is that is incorporated in *When You're Strange*. *HWY* was a movie Morrison made with film pals like photographer Paul Ferrara, who was an acid buddy and our best cameraman," Manzarek recalled in a 2010 phone interview we did upon release of the film.

"I'm one of the Doors on this, and can never watch as simply as one of the Doors. I'm always watching it as a filmmaker. 'How's that cut?' I certainly put my two cents in, and as the process was going along there was a lot of editing changes. I got my way on 90 percent of the changes I wanted to make. There are no talking heads in this documentary."

Gary Pig Gold, 2017
A FILM ABOUT THE DOORS... FINALLY!!

The summer of 1970 was certainly a strange one in, for, and around what we may now quaintly call the pop/rock scene: Paul had just left his Beatles, for starters, the Stones and Dylan were missing-without-much-action, kids were throwing various Jacksons, Osmonds, and even Bobby Sherman way

The Doors at Venice Beach, California, December 20, 1969
Photo by Henry Diltz

up the charts whilst the *older* kids were pretending to get back to the garden via a newly released big-Hollywood *Woodstock* movie.

Meanwhile, yours very truly was busy buying up every single Creedence Clearwater record he could lay his young hands on, I'll have you all know.

Then again there was the, well, *strange* case of John Densmore, Robby Krieger, Ray Manzarek and Jim Morrison who, after having closed out those '60s with a "flop" album (*The Soft Parade*) and even floppier run-ins with the law (their singer having gotten busted acting naughty onstage in Miami, and again on a Phoenix-bound airliner) now found themselves in 1970 under immense pressure to resurrect their career and get back to where they once belonged. As in the basics, musically speaking that is.

These various struggles, conflicts, lewd behavior indictments and *then* some are all fully explored—along with, thankfully, lots of great music too—in a fascinating documentary titled *When You're Strange: A Film About the Doors.*

Now, unlike the band's own series of understandably self-serving concert films over the years or, on *entirely* the other hand, Oliver Stone's utterly cataclysmic 1991 biopic *The Doors*, Tom DiCillo's *When You're Strange* perhaps comes closest to finally presenting, as no less an authority as Ray Manzarek has long promised, "the *true* story of The Doors." It does so by wisely keeping 21st-century interference to a bare minimum, concentrating instead on a wealth of live and studio footage from throughout the band's surprisingly brief career intriguingly intercut with—and this is the film's *real* coup to my eyes—never-before-seen segments from Jim Morrison's barely released 1969 short subject *HWY: An American Pastoral.*

Without ever getting overtly ham-fisted à la the above-mentioned Mr. Stone, DiCillo (along with Johnny Depp's narration) weaves the *HWY* footage of Morrison speeding across the California desert to actually drive *When You're Strange* forward, onward and upward from the band's infant gigs on L.A.'s Sunset Strip through the recording of their debut album in 1966 and subsequent stardom. It's interesting, not to mention important, to realize and understand just how big a *pop* star Jim was at this time: He may have been playing it so cool by singing the dreaded "higher" word when the Doors lit their "Fire" on *The Ed Sullivan Show*, but at the same time this was a man only too happy to appear bare-chested and love-bead-adorned alongside Davy Jones and Mark Lindsay across the pages of *16 Magazine.*

When You're Strange similarly pulls few punches in charting the band's just-as-speedy fall from those poppiest of heights, mainly but *not* fully on account of Jimbo's descent into the depths of alcoholic fear and self-loathing. It was indeed, and still remains, quite disheartening to watch the Doors'

188

slinky frontman decline from the leather-clad Lizard King of every bad girl's Summer of Love dreams to the bearded, bloated ragamuffin who hauled sheep onstage in 1969, only to then berate his audience with cries of "You love it, don't ya? Maybe you love gettin' your face stuck in the shit. You're all a bunch of fuckin' idiots!" Oh, Morrison…

Such performance art with a capital "F" notwithstanding, footage from the band's 1968 European tour, and then a remarkable sequence from the "Wild Child" recording session itself, show the Doors were without a single doubt a *four*-piece band, *oh* so much greater than the sum of its equal parts, with each man contributing his own special brilliance to the creation. There wasn't ever a single weak musical link to this band, its writing, arranging, and (usually) its performing skills, and *When You're Strange* never once lets the viewer get distracted from this critically important fact… despite the carnival atmosphere that never seemed to cease swirling around the entire proceedings.

Finally, we also see how, following that tricky summer of 1970, the band fully rebounded with its final two albums, *Morrison Hotel* and *L.A. Woman* (again, *When You're Strange* presents fabulous footage from the latter's recording sessions… apparently, the last existing footage of the band as a whole).

But then, most inconveniently, Jim moved to Paris and rumor has it actually died there very early on the morning of July 3, 1971.

Now he may indeed remain "hot, sexy, and dead" as *Rolling Stone* declared a decade later, kicking off that Doors Resurrection the band's LLC continues to propagate most efficiently to this day. Yet Tom DiCillo has bravely succeeded, where few have ever even *attempted* to before, in stripping away the excess, puncturing the mythology, and—what a concept!—letting the Doors' MUSIC do the talking.

Strange indeed.

Henry Diltz Interview, 2010

THC Expose magazine

THC Expose: You knew the Doors and did the album cover photo for their *Morrison Hotel* LP. What attracted you to them?

Henry Diltz: They were interesting and weren't a guitar band. They came from a different place. It was that keyboard thing. They didn't have a bass. Ray Manzarek played bass on a keyboard with his left hand. It was a little more classical and jazz-oriented. And then you had Morrison singing those words with that baritone voice. It was poetic and more like a beatnik thing. It was different. And Jim wrote all those deep lyrics. I took photos of them at the Hollywood Bowl in 1968 when they did a concert.

Jim lived in Laurel Canyon. So did Robby and John Densmore. We were all friends in the area. I knew him as a musician just as I was first really taking photos. I did one day with the Doors in downtown L.A. for *Morrison Hotel* and got that picture. Then two days later they needed some black-and-white publicity pictures and we walked around the beach in Venice.

THC Expose: Venice Beach photos has become the image for their recent *When You're Strange* film.

Henry Diltz: Here's the thing. I shot about eight rolls of film that day of them in Venice. Over the years, six or eight of them have become the ones we printed and offered for sales in our gallery. "Here's the beautiful one. Here's the great one. Everyone looks good in this shot." You might look at six or eight in a row and you pick the best one. Someone's eyes are closed in this one. One guy is not looking at the camera. And you pick the one that is great. And that becomes the famous one. Well, somebody at Rhino and the Doors' outfit looked at the proof sheets and found one that did not fit that category. Sort of an outtake.

I never printed it because Jim is not looking at the camera. They are walking and it's not real sharp. But they picked that one and there is something about it. It's random, see. I always picked the ones that look iconic. But really, maybe those random ones in between are kind of more interesting now.

THC Expose: Do you have a theory why the music of the Doors and Laurel Canyon, a region where you lived in 1965–1975, became popular and why the music from that area still resonates in 2010?

Henry Diltz: It was the flowering and the renaissance of the singer/songwriter. I think it had a lot to do with that change that it came from folk music. And then they started putting their own lyrics into it. And smoking grass had a hell of a lot to do with it. Smoking grass had everything to do with the whole '60s thing. Long hair, hippies, peace and love, because that's the way it makes you feel. And love beads and the music. Smoking a little grass makes you very thoughtful and increases your feeling and focus on things. You start thinking about trying to put thoughts into words and songs.

PREVIOUSLY UNRELEASED AND RESTORED FOOTAGE OF THE DOORS UNVEILED; SOUND REMIXED AND REMASTERED BY BRUCE BOTNICK
RecordCollectorNews.com, 2013

On December 3, 2013, Eagle Rock Entertainment released *R-Evolution* from the Doors on DVD, Blu-ray and Digital Formats.

Combining early TV appearances with the Doors' own music films, *R-Evolution* illustrates how the band evolved from the constraints of mid-'60s television to a point where they had the creative input and power to shape how they were portrayed onscreen.

R-Evolution shows the growth of the Doors from being forced to accept the formulaic television approach to taking control of the medium.

R-Evolution brings together a wealth of previously unreleased footage of the Doors. This compilation contains "Light My Fire," "People Are Strange," "Hello, I Love You," "Crawling King Snake," "L.A. Woman," "Moonlight Drive," "Break On Through (To the Other Side)," and many more.

Housed in the collection is a performance of "Break On Through (To the Other Side)" from the Isle of Wight Festival 1970 by director Murray Lerner, a 45-minute documentary titled *The Doors—Breaking Through the Lens, Love Thy Customer*, a never-before-seen 1966 Ford training film with music by the Doors, their television appearances on Dick Clark's *American Bandstand* and one from the Clark-produced TV show *Shebang.* Finally, the DVD has a section of outtakes from the band's appearance on the U.S. TV show *Malibu U* in 1967 and the Doors lip-synching "People Are Strange," with a live Morrison vocal, from the *Murray the K in New York* 1967 TV series.

We now view these clips again in *R-Evolution.*

R-Evolution boasts a wealth of excellent bonus features, including a commentary by Doors members John Densmore, Robby Krieger, and Ray Manzarek, along with Bruce Botnick and Elektra Records founder Jac Holzman.

In addition to the DVD and Blu-ray, a Deluxe Edition is available on each physical format, packaged in a 40-page DVD-size hardback book with a "scrapbook" style presentation on each track including lyrics, background info, trivia and photos.

All footage has been carefully restored to the highest standards, and the sound has been remixed and mastered for 5.1 by Bruce Botnick.

The influential television icon Dick Clark and his weekly *American Bandstand* national television platform first booked the Doors to promote the release of their debut LP.

In a 1999 interview I conducted with Clark for *HITS* magazine, I asked Dick about licensing his valuable archive to film, TV and DVD products. "I wasn't bright enough to know they had historical or money value. But I've always been a collector. I started when I was a child. I saved the returned kinescopes. Now I realize the historical importance of all of this.

"People think that's the file, but it's Chuck Berry, Little Richard, the Crows... It's Jefferson Airplane, the Doors. That's what's so phenomenal about it. I knew it would have entertainment value. I didn't know it would have historical value as well.

"There were not a lot of sources for the early stuff. As time went on, and videos were made and other tape recordings were made of concert appearances, people saved them. So there's more material available. History gets shorter. You can get stuff from the '80s and '90s. '70s is fairly available. '50s and '60s is scarce," Clark admitted.

"In the old days, our interviews with the artists were short. Two to three minutes max. The way I patterned them— I've done 10,000 of them. 10,000 individual interviews. I had what I hoped was a beginning, middle and end. I tried to get something out of it other than 'Where do you go next?' I always tried to get something you could hang on to. Sometimes totally frivolous. Sometimes very stupid. Sometimes not memorable. Maybe just show the humanity. Give them the courtesy of allowing them to get their plug in for a record and then get what you want out of it. It's a very symbiotic relationship. We are using one another," disclosed Clark.

I also asked Dick about the now ancient practice of performers lip-synching their current hits on *American Bandstand*, as evidenced by the Doors clip now incorporated in *R-Evolution.*

Clark endorsed the policy and revealed that at times recording artists lip-synching their songs on live TV could be problematic.

"Oh yeah. I've never relegated the lip-synch to a lower form of entertainment. Lip-synching is an art unto itself. A lot of people can't do it. Jazz singers, improvisational singers just can't pull it off."

THE DOORS' NEVER-RELEASED 1968 SELF-PRODUCED FILM *FEAST OF FRIENDS* OUT ON DVD & BLU-RAY; ALSO INCLUDES U.K. DOCUMENTARY AND RARE FOOTAGE

CaveHollywood.com, 2014

During November 2013, *Feast of Friends*, a never-before-released documentary film on the Doors, produced by the band, was finally commercially released after 45 years.

Shelved due to lead singer Jim Morrison's legal issues, the uncompleted film was only ever seen at a few film festivals and was never completed. Eagle Rock Entertainment, the largest producer and distributor of music programming for DVD, Blu-Ray, TV, Audio and Digital Media in the world, and Doors Property, LLC, have painstakingly remastered the audio and video and compiled bonus footage as well as an historic British documentary called *The Doors Are Open*.

In April 1968, filming began for what would become the first and only film produced about the Doors, by the Doors. Funded by the band and helmed by friend and fellow film graduate Paul Ferrara, the footage shot for this film would become the well from which the majority of future documentaries and music videos about the band would draw.

Paul Ferrara thought it was a great lyric to use for the title. Other than a few appearances in film festivals the following year, an official release of *Feast of Friends* would never be seen. Until now.

"I met and knew Morrison earlier at the Atlanta Film Festival," filmmaker Murray Lerner recollected in a 2010 phone interview. "I was showing *Festival!* It won an award and they had a film they had made played. We talked at the party afterwards, we had both won awards but they were bullshit awards. Mine was for the best music. What does that mean? At the party I really gave it to the organizer out loud a hard time, told him what I felt about him, and they came up to me and said, 'We agree with you.' I got friendly and tried to help them distribute their *Feast of Friends* film."

If not for a poor-quality bootleg copy circulated among collectors and eventually via the internet, the film's existence would have scarcely been known beyond the circle of devoted Doors fans.

By many accounts, the original source of that bootleg is thought to have been Morrison's own copy, which he hand-carried when he relocated to Paris in 1971 after recording what would be the Doors' final album. Concealed in a paper bag and forgotten at a friend's house, Morrison would never reclaim it, as he passed suddenly in July '71.

195

Feast of Friends offers a cinematic look at the Doors on the road during their summer '68 tour. Whilst never truly completed, as the production monies were abruptly cut due to the band's political problems stemming from Morrison's arrest in Miami, the film provides a stylistic approach in true '60s *cinéma vérité* style.

The film is composed of concert performances which are intercut with fly-on-the-wall footage of the group in their natural habitat—playful, sensitive, chaotic and touching. Other than a few bookings in film festivals during 1968, this is the first official release.

Completely restoring from the original negative, Frank Lisciandro helped supervise the edit the film with input by Morrison. The film has been color-corrected and mastered in high definition with the soundtrack totally remixed and remastered by longtime Doors co-producer/engineer Bruce Botnick.

Along with the full version of *Feast of Friends*, this revealing release contains three important bonus features. The first is *Feast of Friends: Encore*. A newly produced feature using footage shot for *Feast of Friends*, *Encore* is a complementary piece that provides a deeper look into the life of the band during this period as they tour, record, travel and even vacation together. The program avoids the typical selection of hits and makes use of the Doors' rare recordings to accompany this unreleased footage.

Encore showcases the band's recording process as the Doors record one of their biggest hits, "Wild Child." Viewers will follow the band as they break from touring to sightsee, play poker in their hotel room and witness an unedited interaction with Jim and the "Minister at Large" who attempts to determine "just what the hell it is [they're] doing."

Fans will also see a newly unearthed solo backstage performance by a singing Robby Krieger, a poem by Jim

Morrison (while, in the background, you can hear Ray Manzarek's piano work on "Love Street"), a never-before-seen altercation with legendary photographer Richard Avedon, a tranquil scene of Jim and his friends at peace in the cool waters of the Kern River, and much more.

The Doors Are Open, a British TV documentary, originally aired on December 17, 1968, focused around the band's performance at London's Roundhouse, which took place just days after the completion of filming for *Feast of Friends*. Interspersed with the band's music are intense scenes from the Vietnam War, political leaders, and riots back in the United States.

The Doors Are Open highlights the political relevance of the Doors' opinionated lyrics and iconic sound while giving context to the tumultuous times in which they were living. Although previously released, the film has suffered from numerous sound and picture quality issues. Now the image quality has been dramatically improved and the sound has been transformed by Bruce Botnick to be as true to the original live sound as possible.

Also included is *The End*—a feature that was filmed in Toronto, Canada, in August 1967. This performance of "The End" was for *The O'Keefe Centre Presents: The Rock Scene—Like It Is*.

It was originally broadcast on October 16, 1967 in Canada, and on August 1, 1970, in the U.S. as part of a musical program called *The Now Explosion*. The selection has an introduction by Noel Harrison and later interviews by John Densmore, Robby Krieger, Ray Manzarek and the Doors' former manager, Danny Sugerman.

This might be one of the best examples of the Doors ever captured on film.

"The concerts were an extension of the audio document," stressed Manzarek to me in a 2010 conversation. "It was not yin and yang. One was an extension of the other."

"There's one really significant fact about the official release of *Feast of Friends*: It's the only movie made about the Doors, and there have been dozens in one form or another, by the band itself—everything else has been produced, edited and distributed by other parties," suggested Doors scholar, Rob Hill.

"In this sense, *Feast of Friends* is exactly how the band saw themselves in 1968. From the spring to the end of summer the band was followed by a film crew as they toured America: getting on and off airplanes, sightseeing on the streets, interacting with fans and acolytes, and, of course, performing onstage.

"Although the film is mainly an abstract *cinéma vérité* series of starts and stops with no real narrative structure—the opening scene is Morrison and journalist Albert Goldman sitting in the back of a limo that deposits Morrison at the back entrance of a concert hall, where he is mobbed by female fans that paw and kiss at him as he bashfully saunters on in his cobra-skin pants; then sharply cuts to the band boarding a monorail in Vancouver; another scene has Morrison talking to a pastor backstage which then bleeds into the band swimming in the Kern River in California; then to the band onstage playing 'The End' at the Hollywood Bowl—the intimacy is clear both on and off the stage.

"And that's because the film was shot by Morrison's college buddies, Frank Lisciandro and Paul Ferrara, while his closest confidante and favorite drinking buddy, Babe Hill, helmed the sound (which, at times, is almost in audible or overdubbed).

"And, most importantly," Hill continued, "Morrison was heavily involved with the editing of the movie along with Lisciandro and Ferrara, even putting up his own money to finish it after the band lost interest and wanted to pull the plug." (Morrison rented a small office in West Hollywood near the Doors' offices so he, Ferrara and Lisciandro would have a place to work.)

"If you feel a sense of déjà vu while watching the film, well, there's a reason for that: Almost all the footage of the Doors used in videos, compilations, documentaries and YouTube vignettes have been mined from *Feast of Friends*, piece by piece.

"Seeing it in its whole, however," countered Hill, "with the color-correcting and sound remixes, is a rush; it was one of the very first of its genre—the rock documentary—naive, experimental and not commercially conscious.

"But the real gems for hardcore Doors fans are the extras, the long-lost treasures from the cutting-room floor, which are almost certainly some of the last unseen footage of the Doors: the band showing up for a photo shoot at the famed photographer Richard Avedon's New York City studio for *Esquire* magazine and Avedon throwing a hissy fit, rushing the camera and telling them they can't film, his hand finally covering the lens; the band sightseeing on Seattle's Space Needle; Morrison improvising on a piano in the bowels of an arena they are waiting to thrill. The camera following a leather-clad Morrison into a backstage dressing room where he recites poetry while holding a still photo of himself onstage at the Fillmore East.

"In short, the extras are a more humanistic, naked and less conscious look at the guys—young men at the height of their success—playing jokes, horsing around and interacting with their fans.

"It's a nice package for any Doors fan trying to wrap themselves around the ever-expansive and debated mythology of the band."

The Doors: Live at the Isle of Wight 1970 on DVD+CD, Blu-ray+CD and Digital Video - article by Harvey Kubernik for CaveHollywood.com, 2018.

The historic last concert ever filmed of the Doors is now available for the first time on February 23, 2018, when Eagle Rock Entertainment proudly presents *The Doors: Live at the Isle of Wight 1970* on DVD+CD, Blu-ray+CD and Digital Video.

The last known unseen performance of the Doors in existence, *The Doors: Live at the Isle of Wight 1970* has been completely recut and remixed from the original film footage. Fully approved by the Doors, this previously unreleased concert was meticulously restored via the latest 21st-century technology, color correcting and visually upgrading the original footage.

The entire concert, which is now presented in 5.1 Dolby Digital sound, was mixed from the original multi-track audio by longtime Doors engineer/mixer/co-producer Bruce Botnick. Fans may have caught a glimpse of this performance in the 1997 Isle of Wight film *Message to Love*; however, this DVD presents the Doors' set with the full-length songs in maximum visual and sound quality.

The scene is August 1970... Frontman Jim Morrison's ongoing obscenity trial, from an incident a year prior in Miami, weighs heavily on the band. "The Last Great Festival" is taking place in England, which boasts a venerable Who's Who of 1970's top acts: Jimi Hendrix, the Who, Miles Davis, Joni Mitchell, Joan Baez and more.... The band touches down on the Isle of Wight. The show must go on.

The Doors: Live at the Isle of Wight 1970 captures and showcases the essence of this poignant performance, as well as offering a snapshot of the era, with footage of fans (more than 600,000 in attendance) tearing down barriers and crashing the gates to gain access to the event.

The Doors hit the stage at 2:00 a.m. on August 30, 1970, delivering a set that further proved the musical power that marked them as a beacon of the Summer of Love. In this 84-minute DVD, Morrison, organist Ray Manzarek, guitarist Robby Krieger and drummer John Densmore traverse such staples as "Roadhouse Blues," "Break On Through (To the Other Side)" and "Light My Fire." Illumination by a mere red spotlight (the band weren't informed that they needed to bring their own lighting equipment) gave the show an eerie crimson hue, almost echoing the figurative weight of the trial.

"Our set was subdued but very intense," Manzarek later stated. "We played with a controlled fury and Jim was in fine vocal form. He sang for all he was worth, but moved nary a muscle. Dionysus had been shackled."

The DVD is completed with bonus featurette *This Is the End*—17 minutes of interviews conducted by the film's original director, Academy Award–winning Murray Lerner with Krieger, Densmore and the Doors' manager at the time, Bill Siddons. Additional archival interview footage with Manzarek from 2002 is also included in the featurette.

In 2013 I interviewed Lerner about his unique camera work capturing the last concert footage on the Doors.

Lerner's *The Other Side of the Mirror—Bob Dylan Live at the Newport Festival 1963–1965, Festival!*, re-released in late 2017, and *Leonard Cohen Live at the Isle of Wight 1970* are essential DVD documents to view and own.

"I've tried to put out the Doors' [1970 Isle of Wight] full set. It was dark, but that was the mood. And the darkness is interesting, I think. Morrison said to me, 'You can film, but you're not gonna get an image. But we're not gonna change our lighting.' 'I'll get an image.' I did.

"I shot color for the Doors, Leonard Cohen and the Isle of Wight performers. It was high-speed Ectochrome reversal. And I'm glad I did it, because the color lasts a lot better in reversal. The camera people I had were with their own cameras for the most part, but they used Arriflexes and Auricon. The main camera used was an Aaton, a kind of avant-garde camera at the time.

"I always use very, very long lenses as an adjunct to my photography. I believe in the long shot because I would like the thing to feel musical and not jumpy. I think film is visual music. And it should be, and I believe in editing that way.

"I personally have a technique where I practice the choreography of the camera. Everyday for about an hour before I shot, having an assistant stand by, and I would focus, zoom and figure out how big the moves had to be to get the result I wanted so I could do it myself. And I practiced all of that. And I kind of instilled that sense of the choreography of the camera being part of the concert.

"For the most part, in the planning stages, I picked positions to shoot. And I told people, 'You concentrate on the close-up and you concentrate on something else.' "

In 2015 I interviewed Tony Funches, the Doors' head of security and Morrison's lone bodyguard, and, in 2017, former *Sounds* magazine journalist Sandy Robertson, who both attended the 1970 Isle of Wight event.

"As I remember it, the Isle of Wight gig was difficult," offered Funches in our 2015 conversation inside the 1967–68 Laurel Canyon home of Jim Morrison. "Late at night, delays, cold weather, 2:00 a.m. and they were not using their P.A. system. They used the [Grateful] Dead's P.A. So they had a hard time getting the sound right on the monitors and stuff, and they soldiered on through it. It was pretty miserable in terms of personal comfort. Not that they wanted to be pampered or anything. It was just dreadful conditions. I was on the stage. When the Doors are onstage, Uncle Tony was there. [Bill] Siddons had one side of the stage and I had the other. They did the gig, and I got to say, the Isle of Wight security was really up to the task and there wasn't really much concern about nitwits come flying out of the audience. Miles Davis stretched out backstage during the set and we all talked later."

"I date my transition to real rock music from my purchase of the sublime *Morrison Hotel* by the Doors, and my subsequent solo trip all the way from Scotland to the Isle of Wight Festival to see them live, age 17," Robertson emailed me in August 2017.

"I had a glamorous older cousin named Linda Gamble (later a music and movie publicist) and she seemed the height of sophistication to me because she took a chance on Love and the Doors when no one else I knew had their records.

"None of my buddies cared about Jim Morrison and company, so I fetched up alone amid crowds of 1970 hippies in scorching summer weather with not even a blanket to my name. I saw the Who, John Sebastian, Kris Kristofferson (who was booed for 'Blame It on the Stones' by irony-free dolts), and Tiny Tim, who sang 'There'll Always Be an England' to the delight of the mob, because he wasn't being ironic at all.

"Night and cold descended, and the Doors didn't appear until the early hours of the morning—Morrison a distant, gleaming blue-black leather figure, his feral growl on 'Break On Through' introduced by Ray Manzarek's sparkling, icy electric piano.

"As Kim Fowley rightly has it, in many ways they were like a jazz group, John Densmore's drum flourishes and Robby Krieger's nimble guitar being just as capable of entrancing the ears as kicking ass.

"The critical consensus seems to be that this was not one of their great shows, Jim having his fragile eggshell mind on legal troubles looming, and indeed, looking at footage of 'Ship of Fools,' Morrison seems like he can hardly be bothered to get the lyrics out.

"Nevertheless, at 17 I came to worship, not to deconstruct, and it was only with age I realized how tough it can be for bands to play the same songs every night while trying to deliver an hour for magic.

"Salvation from the cold was at hand in the form of a cute young girl who let me snuggle under her sleeping bag, alas, however, under the watchful eye of her glowering bro, so there was no chance of romance.

"I left pre-Hendrix as a certain thuggishness was in the air. I arrived home with some dreadful flu-type virus. Never mind—I had seen the Doors open. To this day, when some kid is playing a Doors album in a record store and I mention I'm so old I actually saw Jim Morrison onstage, it's great to feel the excitement bridge the generations to that mystical place where people down there like to get it on, get it on."

Jim Ladd Interview, 2010
THC Expose magazine

I always put the Beatles on their own shelf. But the Doors are the ones who really walked me into the rock 'n' roll lifestyle.

Their first album twisted my brain. I can visualize in my mind, I had been in the hospital with tuberculosis and I had gotten out after four months of isolation. I walked into my friend's hippie apartment. I can see the turntable in my mind, and I'm listening to "Back Door Man." And I went, "Who's that?" And he said, "It's a new band called the Doors." I sat down, lit up a joint and kept putting the album on over and over. I could not stop listening to it. Of course, when I got to "The End," that was it for me.

I was waiting for the Doors to play the Long Beach Sports Arena in February 1970. I was working at KNAC-FM. My mind was blown completely, and by that time they were doing *Morrison Hotel*. I had been a Doors fan since the first album but never saw them. And I went there. This was the days before special effects, pyrotechnics. There was none of that. It was just this band onstage. And they were completely and utterly mesmerizing. It was also, to this day, the tightest band I had ever seen. Right before me, and I thought at the time I knew how to do a segue. They did a medley that would go from one song to another. And until Jim started singing, I didn't realize it. They were that good.

Jim Morrison, Long Beach Arena, 1970
Photo by Henry Diltz

Five years ago a guy in a car called up with a request. And he said, "I've got my son who is 16. He wants to hear some Jimi Hendrix." I still have many people that call me who have been listening since KNAC. Now that's extraordinary. I also have kids who are 16, 17 and 18 requesting Bob Dylan. That's even more extraordinary. They know who the Beatles are and know their music inside and out. They love the Doors.

A kid hearing the Doors' "Peace Frog" today for the first time is going to hear it different than I did because the Vietnam War is not raging. Or the 1968 Democratic Convention with people being beaten up in the streets. However, they are going to hear it in the context of their world. I can't presume to know what that means.

Today I can play that song in the context of today and make it work. So it is still relevant to me because even though it was written back then, I can put it together with something new.

The only thing today's kids are missing is context. I have to keep in mind that the song says something to me but it may say something completely different to someone in the audience. So all I can do it is play it in a way that says something to me, and then how it is interpreted by them in the context of the set, it may be different. If I put the songs together correctly people should recognize, "OK. Morrison is saying something in 'Five to One.' " That's why you have to listen to the lyrics when you listen to my show.

Years ago the recordings of "Helter Skelter," "Peace Frog" and "Gimme Shelter" were warnings and they are reality now. Sometimes the particular or current issue drama will change but the human condition that causes them is the same. The thing that caused war in Vietnam or war in Iraq is war.

It might be more potent now because if you listen to that song it is written about a person, and that person's war. So it's any soldier at any time. Not just the Vietnam War. So that applies to any soldier in harm's way.

I was at my parents' when I got the word in summer 1971 about the death of Jim Morrison. So I went on the air and we were mourning his death when the story broke. You become the public wailing wall. People were calling, first off, to hear it wasn't true. And then they want to spill out their emotions to you. You have to be ready for that while you are doing the show and create this thing. They need to say it to somebody. And you happen to be the person because you are playing all this music.

Dr. James Cushing, 2017

I'm reasonably sure it was the Glendon theatre in Westwood, and it was late July or early August of 1971, and the attraction was a midnight showing of *The Hellstrom Chronicles*, a sci-fi movie about giant insects. I walked into the dark lobby after buying my popcorn, and there they were, sitting on the sofas, wearing rock & roll jeans and T-shirts and jackets, and looking stunned: Ray Manzarek, Robby Krieger, John Densmore, instantly recognizable to a longtime Doors fan.

I was an extraverted 18-year-old who had met his share of celebrities and didn't feel intimidated by genius—plus, I had seen the movie once before (that's why I was there, to see it a second time). So, after saying hi, I thought to ask, "So, have you guys seen this movie before?"

At this point the recollection gets fuzzy, but I remember a brief conversation about this movie, and other movies, in which I felt a glimpse of their shared burden, not as a result of anything said, but of the general tone of voice and facial expressions… I said something like "You enjoy the giant bugs now" before taking my seat.

Tosh Berman, 2017

For some odd reason, the Whisky a Go Go made a decision to have matinee performances for those who are under 21. In other words, a kiddies matinee. Around 2 p.m. my father took me to the Whisky to see the Irish band Them, with Van Morrison.

At the time, I had the first Them album put out by Parrot Records. It had the hits "Gloria," "Here Comes the Night," and the intense "Mystic Eyes." I'm one of those people who not only like to be at the show on time but early as well. I enjoyed being in an audience and watching a room or theater fill up.

I'm that way about movies as well. The theater/audience aspect to me is just as important as the action that will take place on the stage or screen. So, we got there early and we watched and listened to the opening band—the Doors.

The L.A. fab four came on and right away there was something weird about them. For instance, they didn't have a bass player. There was a guitarist, organ player, drummer, and then the singer. The setup was really odd to me. By 11 years old, I know that every band should have at the very least a guitarist, but of course, a bassist is a must as well. I can't remember what their first song was, but the sound that they were playing had a boom-ba-bay sound. It wasn't really rock, and there was a touch of the blues, but to my ears, there was something theatrical about their sound. Like it shouldn't belong to a rock 'n' roll club, but maybe in a theater.

The singer was beautiful. And the rest of the band looked nerdy and academic. For instance, I would not have been surprised that they worked as teachers at the local university—which was UCLA. Down the street from the Whisky (on the Sunset Strip). The one song I did know was "Alabama Song." I know this song by heart because in our family household we have the *Lotte Lenya Sings Kurt Weill* album. Every bohemian family had a copy of this album. So it was a pleasant surprise to hear the Doors perform this song, and on top of that, doing a great version of it.

I could be wrong, but I don't think their first album came out yet. Or as a fact, I didn't have the album, nor have I heard of them before this performance. After getting the album, I realized that they pretty much played every song off this album. Once that LP came out, the Doors were it. There were other "it » bands out there, but the Doors had a weird mixture of Southern California optimism, with dark clouds roaming around the sky and blocking the sunlight. At the time, they struck me as a West Coast band, and not only that but a band from the Westside of Los Angeles. Culver City? Well, clearly

Venice, California. Still, what made them so unique was the ultimate organ sound, which played the bass parts as well.

When I hear the album, they sound like jazz musicians playing rock—or, as I mentioned, not really rock with a roll, but with a theatrical bent, with jazzy overtures. Jim Morrison, their lead singer, could have been a Chet Baker type of singer. He had a beautiful sexy voice. At 11 I sort of knew what sexy was, and I clearly understood that this was Morrison's appeal to the listener.

Them, on the other hand, seemed like they didn't want to play at 3 p.m. in the afternoon. I remember Van Morrison wearing dark sunglasses and not moving a muscle on the stage, except in the mouth area. They sounded great, but compared to the Doors theater, they were blown off the stage by the opening act.

At that age, the Doors represented something dark, adventuresome to me. I went to see them again about a year later at an outdoor concert setting. Somewhere in the San Fernando Valley. Again, it was in the afternoon, and it was really hot and dusty. The Doors set I saw that afternoon was the complete opposite of what I saw and heard at the Whisky. For one, they seemed to have no focus on the stage. They were basically jamming, and Morrison was improvising a lot. Which comes back to the jazz vibe, but here it didn't work. They were boring.

Still, I was a faithful Doors fan. I purchased all their albums from the first to *L.A. Woman* (an album I hated, by the way). People were down on *The Soft Parade* album, but I liked it because of the orchestration, and I feel in a sense that the orchestra and Morrison were a good combination. It's a shame that Morrison didn't become a Broadway or off-Broadway star. He had that vibe, and I think this would have been the suitable platform for his talents. Morrison, I think, wanted to be Artaud, but one can't be an Artaud. Only Artaud is Artaud. Maybe he can do a Michael McClure, but again,

209

there is only one McClure. Which was ironic to me, because McClure eventually did a series of albums and live shows with the organist Ray Manzarek. Which, to my ears, sucked. The reason it sucked was because of the overture of it being a Morrison tribute—and it's weird enough that Morrison wanted to be Michael, but Michael being Jim was absurd to me.

It seems kind of obvious that Morrison knew my father. If for nothing else, due to his friendship with Michael McClure, but alas, they didn't know each other. Still, Morrison wanted my dad to do the album cover for their second album, *Strange Days*. Wallace turned it down, not due to the Doors, but he couldn't deal with the record company insisting on restrictions—like, for instance, having the cover shrink-wrapped, or the band having their name on the cover. The Doors wouldn't have a problem with this, but the record company would go apeshit over my father's demands. I know for instance that he would insist that there would be no sticker price on the cover. When my father does his art, he has complete control. If he didn't get complete control and is not part of the (his) picture, he will turn down the job. Still, the second album is pretty great.

I have seen Jim Morrison twice outside the concert/band format. One time was at the Greek Theater in Los Angeles. We were invited to the show by Neil Young to see , Stills, Nash & Young. As we went backstage, we witnessed Morrison being escorted out by a security guard. He didn't look pissed off—his expression was total indifference. Stephen Stills watched him being thrown out, and I think he tried to stop the security guard, but I think Morrison still had to leave the premises. The other time and very last time I saw him was in Topanga Canyon by the Fernwood Market. He was in a Volkswagen Bug by himself and was drinking from a paper bag.

When Jimi Hendrix died, it was shocking. When Brian Jones died, it was really shocking, because we knew him—but when Morrison passed away in Paris, it didn't seem that weird to me. He kind of left the Doors at the time, or it felt that way. He didn't strike me the type of guy who would come back to a band once he's gone. I think he was doing the romantic poet thing and being in Paris—I mean, who wants to come to West Hollywood and deal with being in the Doors after that lifestyle?

When Morrison died, I pretty much stopped listening to the Doors. I liked every album, except their last one, *L.A. Woman*, due to thinking that the songs were lazy-sounding. They were good songs, because hell, it's the Doors. But they were not advancing to another level. Just marking time. I think after *Morrison Hotel*, they said everything that was possible at the time. So, them splitting wasn't a sad or necessarily a bad thing to me.

What did bug me was the Doors after Morrison passed away. I hated the fact that the organist was making these theories that perhaps Morrison is not dead, and he really spent a great deal of time keeping up with the Morrison legend as much as possible. Teenage stuff. As I became an adult I had no reason to listen to the Doors.

By chance, at my local vinyl store, Mono Records, I found an original mono version of the first album. I played it at home and I was knocked out by the sound coming from one speaker towards the listener. As I write, I'm streaming that album in stereo and it doesn't make it for me. The Doors, at least the first album, has to be in mono or nothing else. Still, the Doors are one of the few bands that didn't make it to my adult ears. I can deal with a lot of music from the era of the 1960s, but the Doors seem flat compared to a band like Love. Now that was a fantastic band. Still, my memory of happiness was playing their albums in my room in Topanga Canyon. That feeling never goes away, but I clearly don't need to relive the experience. Mono was something new to my ears—but, not truly essential in my life right now.

Shepard Fairey Interview, 2012
Treats! magazine

I mean, there's a lot of great stuff that happened in the '60s with rock 'n' roll. I love the Who, Hendrix, Led Zeppelin, a lot of good stuff. I like Cream. I love the Doors. "Peace Frog" might be my favorite track. I do like the Doors a lot. And the fact Ray Manzarek produced the first few X albums.

Classic rock is something I've thought about a lot. Why isn't anybody now making things that seem to have the same weight and the same soul or authenticity? The feeling you get from great music is so abstract it's really difficult to define verbally. But you know when you hear something that is great.

Daniel Weizmann, 2017
Motel Money Murder Madness: Jim Morrison and the Noir Tradition

Some like to make fun of Jim Morrison for his poetic ambitions—he was young, ultra-serious, and at times he had the somber college student's yen for Hamlet-like navel-gazing. What's more, like Michael Jackson and Elizabeth Taylor, the force of Morrison's stardom at times threatens to overshadow his artistic gifts. Patti Smith recently wrote that she felt "both kinship and contempt" watching Morrison perform. But Jim Morrison's lyrics did introduce a whole new and highly literary sensibility to pop music—the Southern California noir of Raymond Chandler and the Southern Gothic tradition of William Faulkner. And pop music has never really been the same since.

Of course, new things were already happening to the song lyric before Morrison made his move: Dylan shocked the airwaves with biblical passion and Whitmanesque frenzy. The Beatles followed with colorful utopian imagery that had roots in James Joyce, Lewis Carroll, and Edward Lear's nonsense verse. But nobody brought the gravity, the hard realism and the psychological pressure of noir to the popular song before Jim. He represented a major leap toward adulthood in '67 and the boomers flipped for it. After a youth saturated with sunshine and goody-goody-gumdrops consumerism, they had secretly been craving just such a counter-move.

The first album's shadowy album cover and billboard, shot by Guy Webster, was a knowing nod to noir film posters like *Out of the Past* and *In a Lonely Place*. And Jim's crooner voice and movie-star good looks defied the rock template, as well. But most of all, the words, their impressionistic, nightmare-like alienation, were strange and yet instantly recognizable.

We can't know exactly what inspired Morrison to fuse the noir dreamscape to the popular song... but he was a military brat, raised in Florida and New Mexico. The South, with its backwoods quiet, its open highways, its malevolence, and its anti-culture, was in his bones. Throw a UCLA dose of Nietzsche, Rimbaud, the exotica of Eastern philosophy, Jungian psych, and the Native American tragedy into the mix, and you've got a potion powerful enough to challenge the lyrical norms as deeply as the sound of Hendrix's guitar did.

One of the last of the Venice Beach beatniks, Morrison self-published slim volumes of verse, even at the height of his rock stardom. He certainly had a hard time straddling his roles as shaman, youth leader, pop icon, and serious artist. But he struggled in earnest, and it's impossible to talk about the Los Angeles tradition that stretches from Chandler, West and Fante to Didion herself, Bukowski and beyond, without seeing Morrison's part.

What's more, for better or worse, whole music genres have Morrison to thank for forging darkness to the pop song. Bowie's Berlin Trilogy, post-punk, and even grunge couldn't have happened without him. Some, like the Cult, seemed only to get the histrionics; others, like Jane's Addiction, reached harder for poetry but lacked the warmth of Morrison's highly intimate voice. Because, in the end, despite the shaman poses, the billboards and the spotlights, Morrison really portrayed himself as a lone human, in true noir fashion, struggling through the night. He wrote from the personal inner space that is poetry.

Celeste Goyer, 2017

Watching the *Doors Live at the Bowl* live show on DVD reminded me of the really essential shamanic quality of that group. The three band members doing everything that created this atmosphere that I don't think has been heard since that day by a band.

They are an art band. Because of the intelligence of the band members and their background. Jim Morrison was involved in the world of literature and poetry and was serious. You can hear a Doors song and it takes you and traces you in many directions and it goes deep. So these were not ordinary rock 'n' roll lyrics. The individual members all had contributions to make beyond what was already made by someone in their role.

Is it sexy? Yes. Both Jim Morrison and Raymond Manzarek are highly effective in that rock 'n' roll sex way. However, it also tied in art and poetry in such a way that it captured a wide audience. And it's not just rock 'n' roll. And it's been more durable. The ability I think is involved comes from the originality and the archetypical quality of their work. The lyrics and the music. And nobody has done anything like it since.

And also the limitations. Because they didn't have the bass player. Once again, limitations create openings. And they wouldn't have sounded that way if they had gone more conventional with their instrumentation. The two-handed organ work is the Doors' sound and it's still effective.

When Morrison stepped away from the image and photos of the first few albums, grew a beard, gained weight, he wanted to be documented in that way. The same way that Dylan tried to step aside from being the spokesman of the generation. Morrison didn't want to be limited or defined by his initial role he created that was successful. That was gonna happen whether he lived or not.

Michael Macdonald, 2017

In four short years the Doors released six studio albums that all had something to offer, including the oft-maligned *The Soft Parade*; however, it was their final offering, *L.A. Woman*, that registered with me more than the others. I had just turned 15 when *L.A. Woman* was released and beginning to appreciate music way beyond radio fare, which may explain why the album still resonates with me. That and Jim Morrison's death shortly after its release probably make *L.A. Woman* even more poignant.

Had Morrison lived, the album would have been regarded as transitional, as the Doors were reaching back into the blues and had severed their connection with regular producer Paul Rothchild. Virtually self-produced, *L.A. Woman* was housed in a rather nondescript cover with a standard band photo revealing a portly and bearded Morrison almost unrecognizable from the lithe rock god of the late '60s. Sound-wise, it was mostly lean and bluesy, while Morrison's lyricism, particularly on the title track and the closing "Riders on the Storm," seemed much closer to Ross Macdonald than Rimbaud.

Australia embraced *L.A. Woman* as they had the Doors' previous albums and gave "Love Her Madly" (a song almost tailor-made for Tom Jones or Chris Farlowe) and the brooding

Greg Franco, 2015

"Riders on the Storm" heavy radio rotation. Forty-five years on, both songs are regularly played on Aussie classic-rock stations, and on any Saturday night at any suburban beer barn, the resident cover band, more often than not, will be cranking out "Roadhouse Blues" (from the equally fine *Morrison Hotel*) or taking collective requests for it. Australia's love for the Doors has never diminished.

Where the Doors would have gone after *L.A. Woman* is purely academic. Morrison may have ventured into spoken-word recordings or become an independent filmmaker. He might have kept the Doors going well into the late '70s, or maybe ennui would have set in. Whatever the direction, it would have been nice if he'd stuck around a lot longer.

Greg Franco, 2015

I was purposefully walking down Chapel Street in Melbourne, Australia, going to our Rough Church gig Wednesday right before Easter in 2012.

Being in a city new to you, playing your original music was the kind of experience one hopes for in a lifetime.

For a brief moment I stopped outside a bar where there was a movie projected on a screen. The movie looked cool. It was in black and white, and there was a band playing on the screen.

The shot switched to this guy being interviewed. I snapped a photo, figuring it was a cool thing to capture. I filed it away in my mind: Chapel Street, Prahran, Melbourne, Australia, 2012.

A year later at home, I looked closer at my "artier" trip photos, and one was of this guy being interviewed. It was

Ray Manzarek. It hit me like a ton of bricks, wow. Ray had just died.

It seemed an important coincidence.

There is this fascination with Jim, and I get that. Everyone was into Jim. If you were a dude from his generation, you had to see him as one of the most fascinating people on the planet. He was a shaman, a sex god, a total mess, everything. Drummer John Densmore and guitarist/songwriter Robby Krieger were essential components. But as I got older, and I saw how this all played out, Ray became the focus. No doubt the Doors needed a muse man, but they also needed a focused genius to make rock history.

Ray went on to produce X's first album, and that is a musical touchstone of my generation. If you think you know something about Los Angeles rock music and you don't know this album, then you are sadly out of touch.

X's *Los Angeles* was my generation's wake-up call; let's burn all the classic-rock records now! (But never the Doors records.) Ray figures into that important musical history. Hell, he played his ass off on that record.

The Doors are the best band from this town, with a little plug for X and Minutemen. The Doors are our tribal elders, heady art and film guys with burning dark souls. They got down with badass beat poets, psych rock, blues and jazz. They built that legacy for us out of the Los Angeles soil, sand and rock. They changed music for all time.

Why did this happen? It's just in the water, baby. Los Angeles is a Mecca. We have our glorious heroes, and it will always be that way.

Ray Manzarek, December 20, 1969
Photo by Henry Diltz

Ray Manzarek A Tribute
Harvey Kubernik, 2013
CaveHollywood.com

Ray Manzarek, keyboardist and the co-founder of the Doors, died May 30 at the age of 74 in Rosenheim, Germany, of bile duct cancer. Manzarek is survived by his wife Dorothy, son Pablo, and grandchildren Noah, Apollo, and Camille.

Ray cared deeply about music, the Doors, art, cinema, the UCLA basketball team, his family, and our planet.

He loved Jody Maroni sausages and his Indian food served very spicy.

"Ray Manzarek was a rock 'n' roll scholar," summarized Kim Fowley.

"Ray Manzarek was *Goodbye Mr. Chips* as a young man and he never grew old. Ray Manzarek was from Chicago. So he understood *Studs Lonigan* and he understood Chess Records and he probably understood Riley Hampton. Google him, folks. Ray Manzarek understood Vee-Jay Records. He must have understood Calvin Carter. He knew who Jerry Butler was. Just as important, Ray Manzarek knew where Europe was, he knew where Asia was, and he knew where he fit into the solar system.

"Ray Manzarek from the very beginning to the very end was an immaculate-attired gentleman. He had his own sound, his own worldview and his own perception of what was surreal, real and unreal. We always got along well. We never recorded together. But we would speak sometimes in the shadows about the sunlight that we weren't missing.

"Ray Manzarek will be missed. Somewhere in heaven Ray is playing music and the band has already improved their sounds since he joined."

"Ray Manzarek is the 'forgotten man' in the history of jazz-rock fusion," observed Dr. James Cushing. "Months before Miles Davis began experimenting with electric keyboards, and years before the Tony Williams Lifetime, the Doors' organ-guitar-drums trio sound opened secret passageways between rock and jazz. The great traditions of Jimmy Smith, Richard 'Groove' Holmes and Big John Patton may have been under the radar of rock 'n' roll radio, but Ray Manzarek knew that music well.

"I propose that another secret may have been this: Percy Rimbaud was backed up by the Richard 'Groove' Holmes Trio disguised, Superman/Clark Kent style, as UCLA white boys. Of course, one can push this connection too far. Holmes, Jimmy Smith, Jack McDuff and the rest all swing in a way the Doors do not, and the soul-jazz sensibility relates more to Gershwin and Cole Porter than to William Blake and Howlin' Wolf. And many Doors tracks use bass guitar instead of organ bass pedals.

"But listen to the bigger picture. Soul-jazz represented a hip and profitable compromise between mainstream music and "minority" culture. 'Groove' Holmes made the *Billboard* Top 50 in 1965 with 'Misty,' and Grant Green did a samba-flavored cover of 'I Want to Hold Your Hand' the previous year. Both those cuts feature drum patterns I hear Densmore varying in 'Break On Through (To the Other Side).' Furthermore, both Manzarek and Jimmy Smith were equally convincing playing blues and making noise (dig Smith's 'The Champ'). And it's a short step from the shimmer of the Doors' 'End of the Night' to Miles Davis's 'In a Silent Way.' "

"Look, it's not a white band. It's a black and white band, it's white guys infused with jazz," is how Ray once described the Doors in a nosh we had at Greenblatt's Delicatessen in West Hollywood 20 years ago.

"You see, nobody came here to make it. Jim and I came to go to the UCLA film school, and John and Robby are natives. Westside boys who surfed, for God's sake. The Doors were never part of the folk-rock country-rock laid-back 'Peaceful Easy Feeling' of Los Angeles. The Doors were part of Raymond Chandler, John Fante, Dalton Trumbo. It was the dark streets and *The Day of the Locust,* ya know. *Miss Lonely Hearts.* That's where the Doors come from. The Doors are L.A., the beach and downtown L.A.

"I've been doing music since I was 8 years old," Manzarek explained to me in a 1974 conversation at Mercury Records in Hollywood for *Melody Maker.* "I was trained classically and I think it opened up a lot of avenues for the rock element to enter. Rock 'n' roll to me is just like jazz. It's an improvisational medium.

"I left classical music because it didn't allow me to improvise," emphasized Ray. "I didn't feel that I wanted to subjugate myself to another man's thoughts. I loved the technical training, though, and there's nothing like it. I love the act of making my fingers move over the organ and piano.

"The whole Doors organ sound, what makes that work, that's my whole Slavic upbringing. That's being a 'Polish pianist.' That's that dark Slavic Stravinsky, Chopin, that great mournful Bartok-type thing. Dark, mournful Slavic soul married so perfectly with the Carson McCullers American Florida Southern Gothic words 'Tennessee Williams' poetry, that the two of us went 'Crunch!' and the whole thing came right together perfectly. Playing with Jim, Robby and John was falling off a log. Writing those songs and inventing things.

"The Doors… Each song and album has its own place. I still play the albums and can live the emotion. A lot of beautiful times went down. I think of going to UCLA, meeting Jim, meeting Dorothy Fujikawa, who's now my wife, and a lot of great times.

"That was such a fecund time, as Jim said: In that year we had a great visitation of energy. That year with the Doors lasted from 1965 to 1971. We were just composing fools. So that was the easiest thing I've ever done," concluded Raymond Daniel Manzarek with a beatific smile.

The Doors, Venice Beach Pier, California, December 20, 1969
Photo by Henry Diltz

ABOUT THE AUTHOR

**Harvey Kubernik, 1982
KLOS-FM La Cienega Blvd,
Los Angeles, California
Photo by Anton Kline,
(Harvey Kubernik Archives)**

Harvey Kubernik, is a native of Los Angeles and a child of Hollywood California. He's the author of 14 books. Including *Leonard Cohen Everybody Knows, Neil Young Heart of Gold, Canyon of Drea*ms *The Magic and the Music of Laurel Canyon, It Was Fifty Years Ago Today the Beatles Invade America and Hollywood*, and 2017's *1967 A Complete Rock Music History of the Summer of Love.*

His most recent title, a literary music anthology *Inside Cave Hollywood: The Harvey Kubernik Music InnerViews and InterViews Collection, Vol. 1* was published in January 2018 by Cave Hollywood.

In fall of 2018, Sterling/Barnes and Noble will publish *The Story of the Band 1966-1976* a collaboration by Harvey and Kenneth Kubernik.

Over his 45 year music and pop culture journalism endeavors, Harvey Kubernik has been published domestically and internationally in *The Hollywood Press, The Los Angeles Free Press, Melody Maker, Crawdaddy, Variety, The Hollywood Reporter, Billboard, Shindig!, MOJO, The Los Angeles Times, Ugly Things, Record Collector News* magazine, cavehollywood.com and rocksbackpages.com, among others.

223

Kubernik is a record producer, a radio, film, television and Internet interview subject and a former West Coast Director of A&R for MCA Records. He has penned the liner notes to the CD releases of Carole King's *Tapestry*, Allen Ginsberg's *Kaddish*, *The Elvis Presley '68 Comeback Special* and The Ramones' *End of the Century*.

Kubernik serves as Contributing Editor of *Record Collector News* magazine and displays articles and essays on cavehollywood.com on a monthly basis.

In November 2006, Kubernik was invited to address audiotape preservation and archiving at special hearings called by The Library of Congress held in Hollywood.

During July, 2017, Harvey Kubernik was a guest speaker at The Rock & Roll Hall of Fame's Library & Archives Author Series in Cleveland, Ohio discussing *1967 A Complete Rock Music History of the Summer of Love*.

A full literary and music biography of Harvey Kubernik's 45 year music journalism journey, current century activities and upcoming 2018 ongoing work is available on Kubernik's Korner at otherworldcottageindustries.com.

BIBLIOGRAPHY

This is Rebel Music.   Harvey Kubernik, University New Mexico Press, Albequerque, New Mexico, 2004.

Canyon of Dreams The Magic and the Music of Laurel Canyon. Harvey Kubernik, Sterling, New York, New York, 2009.

1967 A Complete Rock Music History of the Summer of Love. Harvey Kubernik, Sterling, New York, New York, 2017.

CPSIA information can be obtained
at www.ICGtesting.com
Printed in the USA
BVHW041301210720
584239BV00013B/111